CAME TO OXFORD

Oxford Morning

GERTRUDE BONE

Came to Oxford

Illustrated by
MUIRHEAD BONE

'*Came to Oxford, a very sweet place*'
PEPYS

BASIL BLACKWELL
OXFORD ⌐ MCMLIII

FIRST PUBLISHED 1952
REPRINTED 1953

PRINTED IN GREAT BRITAIN IN THE CITY OF OXFORD
AT THE ALDEN PRESS

PLATES PRINTED IN COLLOGRAVURE BY HARRISON & SONS LTD.
LONDON, HAYES AND HIGH WYCOMBE

BOUND BY THE KEMP HALL BINDERY, OXFORD

Dedication

'Are you related, Sir, to a tall young gentleman who used to come to this garden a good deal? Very interested in the plants and birds, he was. We had many a talk together. I showed him what I wouldn't have shewn to many people, where the fire-crest had her nest. He used to watch her feeding on the teasels. Very pleased he was. He was always studying. He used to sit on that seat first and then move to that one. His mother used to meet him here sometimes. And then he never came again. I thought he must have gone abroad. . . .'

'Nor sorrow comes; nor tears; nor tired old age.'

Acknowledgment

My thanks for help must be genial and wide-spread. To Mr. Steven Watson of Christ Church for reading my manuscript and prophesying well of me. To Dr. Charles Holden, F.R.I.B.A., for smiling on my architectural excursions. To Mr. J. B. Segal of the School of Oriental Studies, London University, for pointing out many years ago the cryptogram hidden in the Hebrew inscription on the wall of the Botanic Garden, and later furnishing for me its solution. To Mr. Charles Mitchell of the Warburg Institute, London University, for suggestions about the Solomonic pillars, and to Mr. H. M. Last, Principal of Brasenose, for permission to include the Grace recited at the Gaudy dinner in the College. My husband's drawings generate their own gratitude.

Contents

Plates

*T*HREE *things are to be observed saith the approved Dr. Burley concerning a city.*
   I.   That it be healthful in the north part.
   II. That in the easte it be plaine and open.
   III. That on the south and west it be hilly.

Even as Oxford, saith he, was by the industrie of the philosophers from Greece ordained and appointed. And indeed, for such a site, Oxon may compare with any of her sister-cities within this land. The hills which are upon her south and west part and partly on the north-east side, what greater ornaments can there be for her situation: forasmuch as they have bin and are partly still loyned with woods.

The plaines which are on the east and the south-east and north part, what more commendable! When at the welcome season of the year they are gloriously mantelled with a delightful verdure, and the winding rivulets which are therein seen from the hills above to the prying spectator as soe many snakes disporting themselves therein.

These are the incomparable conveniences of nature and art that have inticed kings, queens and princes to retire here for refreshment and diversion, and to have built their pallaces bothe in and neare it.

These (with the University), are those inducements that have drawne the representatives of the nations here in several ages. And such also are the delights that invite foreigners from a far to receive them.

I

The Dreaming Spires

Porter (to old lady travelling with pets).
Please 'M, Station-master says 'M, cats is dogs and rabbits is dogs and so's parrots, but this ere
tortoise is a hinsect and there ain't no charge for 'im.

Punch — C. KEENE's *drawing*

SHOULD not the grey towers of Oxford first steal upon one's consciousness with solemn music and the grave melody of ancient chimes; the dreaming spires but deepen the shadows of antiquity within the ancient trees? It would be seemly. Yet it was the clacking of bright green shoes and the scuffling, darting and nosing of a little mongoose being taken for an airing in the water-walks of Magdalen that gave me the first surprising sensation of being at last in such a place as I had never been in before. And I was inviting romance too, having gone to seek poetry in the Poet's Walk, and having all round me that golden autumn in which the towers and gardens glow like mellow fruit in their bright-rimmed meadows.

The sunlight entered the grove, keeping me company among the trees. Their fallen leaves coloured the banks, their thinning branches revealed the streams (green veins in the hollows) and I was watching the shadows turn blue where the water slid under the bridge, when I first became aware of the green shoes and the astonishing mongoose.

The mongoose was visible all at once, but the green shoes (emerald and shining), were only the base of a lady, who was, it appeared, longing for conversation.

The little grey creature, which she held on a leash, snuffed and scuffled and darted to the utmost of its liberty.

'He's *so* convenient you know,' said the lady, '*such* a good pet and *so* convenient for travelling! You see I don't have to pay for him on the railway. I should have to take a ticket for a dog, but I just slip the mongoose in my pocket and no one knows he's there. I haven't to pay his fare or anything! Don't you think he's a good pet?'

A little bewildered, I supposed he was; but the mongoose, taking advantage, pulled at the lead, and the green shoes, jerked suddenly, had to follow.

It was certain to me from that moment that I had never, in any English city I was ever in, met a grey mongoose being taken out for a walk, and it was clear that I must revise my expectation of the city of Oxford, must weave another pattern for my filigree-work of romance.

That was, however, only the beginning of my astonishment when I came to inquire into this matter of Oxford, its city and its students. The imaginations of many centuries have had their way with its history and its fortunate youth. Some have written of her as those, who, in doing so, lay a wreath upon their own fair and vanished boyhood. Some have the scholar's concern that things should be clearly and properly related. They would forestall insidious errors in fact. There is a great looking backward in any book upon Oxford and I have read this, that, and the other civic and academic record, and many authors upon her achievements and renown. But my last astonishment still remains my final one, when, in reading a discourse upon the charms of Oxford in the year 1608 by a priest called Fitz-Herbert, I found that the simplicity of the gentleman's imagination had lit upon the pleasant fancy that, from her situation on the map, Oxford might be, and indeed was, the *umbilicus* of England.[1] But perhaps he was only repeating Tradition and the Mabinogian was his authority. Let antiquity speak! 'And the second plague,' said Llevelys, 'behold it is a dragon and another dragon of a foreign race is fighting with it, and striving to overcome it. And therefore does your dragon make a fearful outcry. After thou hast returned home, cause the island [Britain] to be measured in its length and breadth, and in the place where thou dost find the exact central point, there cause a pit to be dug, and cause a cauldron full of the best mead to be put in the pit with a covering of satin and thou wilt see the dragons fighting in the form of terrific animals . . . and some time after this Lludd caused the island to be measured in its length and breadth. *And in Oxford he found the central point* and in that place he caused the earth to be dug.'

Coventry, it seems, has also claimed this curious distinction, but, for me, the dragons win.

---

[1] 'Dividitur omnis Anglia in quinquaginta unum comitatus sive Provincias, quorum medium locum tanquam umbilicum obtinet comitatus Oxoniensis, eiusque caput Oxonia civitas.'

Eights Week: Between the Races

The Shining Mile

The far-famed Citty Oxford, being sweetly hugged in ye pleasant arms of those 2 pure rivers, ye Tems and ye Cherwell, whose timely floods enrich ye meadows with excellent herbage.

THOMAS BASKERVILLE, *Account of Oxford* (1670–1700)

IT must be a very early impression I carry of the 'Citty Oxford' that whenever or wherever one reached a boundary, there also one arrived at water — water of river, of stream, of canal or even flood. So that, in my memory, Oxford fills a place like Sulmona, 'abounding in waters'; save that the waters of Oxford are not rushing and leaping like those of the Abruzzi, but flooding and quiet. Even the names of the rivers around it are gentle and sweet-sounding — Evenlode, Windrush, Colne, Cherwell — names, one thinks of the plains, not of the hills, and the trees which follow the winding of the rivers are also of the valley, the willows of Hinksey, the alders of the meadows, the poplars of the Isis. It certainly is a fact that one never finds a quiet green place on the margin of Oxford without encountering there the slipping and glancing of water, its cool and its quiet.

Yet I have only heard of one modern traveller who came to Oxford by way of the river, and she was a lady from South Africa who disembarked at London and came up the Thames to Oxford expressing great pleasure in the diminutive glories of our English river; for, in spite of chatter and noise to the furthest highway of England, the incredible hush of the Thames still winds past Oxford to the sea.

'I *am* going to London,' said a gentleman in the train; 'but perhaps it will surprise you to learn that I am going part of the way by river. I am leaving the train at Reading and going by river to Windsor. I always find that reach of the river the finest. I shall take all day to get to London,' he added brightly as he closed the door behind him.

But these are exotic figures of the present. The ancient river by which so much water-borne trade came and went has become, like the Norfolk Broads, a pleasure-pool of youth.

It is only when one becomes aware how few roads and how many water-ways approach the city, that one sees Oxford as the historians describe it, a wooden town surrounded by hilly forest and marsh, vulnerable from the sea, its rivers the easiest way of approach for enemy as well as friend; for mariner bringing fish, and merchant corn and meat; later see the barges coming up the Cherwell ('Nothing but rain now hinders the coming of the barges', 1608) for the seventy looms working on Parry's

Mead, and the market-produce paying toll at Hythe Bridge Wharf, before being carried up Great Ditch (George Street) to the market at Carfax. One understands early lawsuits about the toll of fish for the Abbots, and the statutes to keep the tributaries free from pollution, and to regulate the size of fish to be caught. One sympathizes with the Mr. Mayor of 1641: 'Forasmuch as some of the ffisherman in St. Thomas' parishe and elsewhere doe much neglect Mr. Mayor by not serving of ffishe unto him in the lent time accordinge to an ancient custome. It is therefore agreed that those persons which have soe neglected Mr. Mayor, shall not be suffered to ffishe in the Citte waters untill a month after T'other ffishermen, who did bring ffishe to Mr. Mayor have fished.'

One reads how much cheaper carriage by barge than by wagon, and understands something of the importance of the river to the trade of the city, from its records. In 1620 for instance 'It is agreed that this Citty shall joyne with the Universitie in equall charge at this present parliament for procuring the former acte for bringing the barges to Oxford and making the ryver navigable, to be amended in poynts of defect.' Even today, the annual beating of the bounds of the City includes a good many water-jumps.

It is the tideless basin of the canal which now brings its water-borne trade and coal to Oxford, and one sails the Isis and the Cherwell for their blessed cessation of noise. Nenuphar and flag still grow in peace; moorhens nest in tranquillity; reeds bow with the same inclination as in the days of Midas; willows drip golden fountains in the winds and herons beat down the distance of the sky over solitary marshes. For refreshment of the eye with green and silver and the long hush of its reaches, it is worth sailing the Thames (even from South Africa).

But it is to the shining mile where the ancient state barges of the London river seem to have sailed to the Isis and liked it so well that they have stayed there ever since, that the eyes of the ambitious are turned. There are, as I said 'a plenty' of rivers round Oxford. There are backwaters where alder and willow almost cover the stream and one can spend summer afternoons very happily in the flat-bottomed punts of ease.

But these are the lilies and languors of the river. The Shining Mile is stern endeavour.

(To forestall any remonstrance from earnest people, I chronicle the fact that the length actually rowed by the College Eights is one mile and two furlongs.)

'Rugby? Oh you mean to play Rugby? Well, of course, I've nothing against Rugby. It's a nice little game. But remember! *A College stands by its boats!*'

You are impressed by that visit of the great Captain of Boats. You join the band of consecrated oarsmen sitting apart at table. You eat next-to-raw beef steaks. No smokes! No drinks! 'The College stands by its boats!'

You frequent the river. I have a fancy for it on a winter morning of frost shining in sunlight. From one of those ancient narrows for defence called a gut you look on a silver river at pause. The towing-path is empty. The free ferry crosses a gleam with the gravity of Time on a dial. You look back and forth at that bend in the path and see a clear and empty river shining and waiting, the shining mile of hope lying under the willows with their threatening fists. And all the Term, for you the river bears the weight (rolling smooth again after washing high up to the roots of the willows) of the splashing and striving of boats —*your* boat!

Your muscles ache! You patiently endure a good deal of flyting from an irascible coach on a bicycle. You steady your stroke; your leg-work improves; a grunt of approbation heartens you for a week. Term goes by and you can do nothing else. You begin to wish you hadn't —and then it comes! mastery over those difficult paces, easy muscle, conquered breathing! You walk like a person apart and precious. Nothing less than the shining mile for *you*!

It's nervous work when it comes; when the boat swings out from the barge and you settle your legs and strike water under the eyes of the elegancies in appropriate costume, and the other men of the College.

The elegancies you don't mind so much. After all they are probably more afraid of you than you are of them. But the appraising eyes of the other men and other crews —these are the formidable tests. 'The College stands by its boats!'

Once out on the shining mile you are spared the laments of the longshoremen that the Eights 'isn't what it was!' 'Why! *I* can remember the time when there was bands playing and they trimmed the barges up with flowers. Hundreds, thousands, there was! It's nothing like it was in my young days.' You don't hear how the weather is always bad at the Eights —'of course today's an exception!'

You hear nothing of these disclaimers as you measure your shining mile —three heart-beats to two strokes, a difficult rhythm. They are beautiful things these swallow-tapered boats and not all longshoremen are captious. I was peering through a certain railing which gives a long sight of the boats when Oriel swung past —a boat and crew who had found themselves and were everything that a College longs for in the way of rowing, when I heard a voice chanting beside me, and all for its own pleasure too, not in the least for my information, 'A lovely crew! That's lovely rowing! A lovely crew that is!' If the gentleman had been Welsh (perhaps he was) I should have said that the delight of his subject had brought him into the *Hwyl*, for he sang on in a fine afflatus till they were past.

For a sight of the finish and beauty of water-craft wait for the parade of the golden boats at the end of the Eights, and after it is all over except a few belated pistol-shots to carry you on to the next Eights week, slip under the alders and beech beside the Cherwell and see the apotheosis of all that is charming in English rivers. Perhaps just because I was not expecting it, the sight seemed to me especially delightful. The sunlight slanted over the buttercup-meadows of Christ Church and the whitethorn shook all its fragrance into the light. Scarlet thorns, heavy to the ground with blossom, made a quiet brilliance on the green bank of the river. Foundations of beryl and jasper lay in the water by the tunnel of birch and alder when the returning punts broke through. By ones and twos at first and then in a medley they came, drawn, it seemed, by teams of coloured balloons and urged on by the gay voices of girls. They drew homeward and away and as I watched them I thought that the return of the punts from the last of the Eights on that superb evening of May, one of the prettiest sights I had ever seen in England.

III

'1826'

'THE girls rowed their College barges up and down the river'? I think probably not; but there were other people who did. The decoration on the cover of the *Illustrated London News* is the only current print known to me in which there is perpetuated the kind of State Barge which one day set out from London manned by the Lord Mayor's watermen to row to Oxford. (Notice in the print the gondola-like prow of the barges made to accommodate rowers.)

I had surmised that all the barges on the Oxford shore had once been of this fleet of London Companies, and had found, after service on the Thames, an honourable retirement to the Isis. But I was wrong. There were many sales of barges from the City Companies to the Oxford Colleges. The Exeter barge was even returned on loan now and again to the Stationers Company from which it had been bought for such an occasion as the Lord Mayor's procession of state barges on the Thames at London (see cover of *Illustrated London News*). But no original barge of any City Company remains now at Oxford. The dwindling company still afloat is in replica.

Now and again these slip their moorings. If, for instance, a College boat took part in the Regatta at Henley, its Barge chaperoned it thither in some motherly splendour; and an expedition by Barge in the nineteenth century seemed nothing out of the way. American Consul Nathaniel Hawthorne writes of Oxford: 'We reached Folly Bridge, Oxford. Here we took possession of a spacious barge with a house in it; and a comfortable dining-room or drawing-room within the house, a level roof on which we could sit at ease or dance if so inclined. These barges are very common at Oxford — some very splendid ones being owned by the students of the different Colleges, or by clubs. They are drawn by horse, like canal-boats; and a horse being attached to our barge, he trotted off at a reasonable pace, and we slipped through the water behind him with a gentle and pleasant motion, which, save for the constant vicissitude of cultivated scenery was like no motion at all. It was life without the trouble of living.'

But the Lord Mayor of London outdid him, for it ran in his mind one day in the year 1826 to visit the Mayor of Oxford and return by way of the Thames. Having, himself and his alderman, to inspect the river in the course of ceremonial duty and to claim prerogatives over a reach on the Middlesex side, and the London Mark Stone of their goal being near Staines, it seemed a possible and adventurous thing to include a visit to Oxford. A modest excursion was at first proposed, just accommodation at inns in Oxford for the party, and a dinner at night in Oxford for the Mayor and magistrates of that city. The London adventurers would return to London by the evening of the following day. It seemed all very nervous work. But it was all put down and the Lord Mayor's chaplain wrote the history.

'If it were not notorious how soon the rumour of any measure is propagated, even before it is fully matured, it would be almost incredible that this excursion should have scarcely been determined upon in London before it was known in Oxford.' A handsome invitation from the Mayor of Oxford followed. 'A pleasing sort of embarrassment' was felt by the Lord Mayor and Aldermen of London. They were bent on entertaining and here they were to be entertained!

From this difficulty they were happily released by the question 'Could not your Lordship go a day sooner to Oxford?' This, it was soon seen, 'would obviate every difficulty'. They could dine and be dined. And they would return to London by the City State Barge, which, already being taken to Oxford under direction of Mr. Saunders, the water bailiff, 'expended five days in its passage thither'.

It was all settled so. Ladies were of the party, and the chaplain went to say grace and write the story. (His story is in the high manner, for there was more than one state banquet, and beyond the fact that the feasts were all that could be wished, we hear not a word of what they had to eat!) There were, however, feasts for the mind and we enter Oxford by road with appropriate emotion. 'You feel,' writes the excellent man, 'the moment you have crossed the stone bridge and are passing the row of rugged elms that overshadow the pathway in front of Magdalen tower — that you are now more exclusively within the solemn realm of literature where learning, which in other places is contented to lodge in cottages or to be closetted in garrets, dwells here in palaces and puts on all the pomp and circumstance of majesty.' After that it is not surprising to learn that Oxford, University as well as Civic Dignitaries, rose to the occasion. The journey was made by land coach. Ladies accompanied the expedition and to these the *Loving mother* extended her sheltering (and delicate) arm. Learned fare was provided and the Regius Professor of Medicine showed how it should be done.

'Among the principal preparations which the Professor's kindness exhibited — and which are all so elegantly constructed, as in no degree to offend the delicacy of the most refined female mind — was a portion of the alimentary canal of the turtle, showing the arteries and veins artificially filled with wax, and the absorbent vessels with quicksilver.'

Folly Bridge and Christ Church meadows have seen many companies of spectators, but seldom can so gay a sight have been offered to them as the start of the Lord Mayor of London's State Barge for its journey to London 'in the month of July 1826'.

A pother of boats hung round the Barge, and the shallop of the Thames Navigation Company carried important people. Another large boat held the Yeomen of the Household and here, oblivious of the fact that 'every spot that could contain a face or a footstep was aware of him', the cook was already at work preparing a fire 'in a grate fixed in the bow of the boat'.

Ten scarlet silk banners on the barge; the City Watermen in scarlet liveries — crowds acclaiming all the way to London (the party stayed one night at Reading and another at Windsor) the ringing of bells, the saluting of guns, that was the way Lord Mayors did things in 1826. Once away from the towns and seriously addressed to the task of getting to London, the state barge with its rising and dipping oars must have been a brave sight winding through green fields and followed by bowing reeds — a resplendent pageant of London floating loose on the Thames — a town-gallant showing himself in the country!

But surely the crowd at the water's-edge expect something from the Lord Mayor himself, for it seems to be, not the Barge (perhaps such a vessel was a more ordinary sight then than now) — but The Right Hon. William Venables, Lord Mayor of London, whom everyone has come to see. He has a pretty wit. Two figures of fun on broken-down rusty ponies shambled along the road to look at the procession and the Lord Mayor has his joke. One of them he hails, flings him a piece of money (*How* they did things!) and tells him to make haste to the Bear Inn, Reading, and order the Lord Mayor's carriage to meet the barge at Caversham Bridge. Sancho Panza, belabouring his pony, slipping first from one side of the saddle to the other, knees up to the pony's mane, did his errand. The Lord Mayor's carriage *was* waiting at Caversham Bridge!

But it was when the 'civic flotilla' arrived at Cliefden that his Lordship 'was in the immediate neighbourhood of his paternal fields'. On this visit, it seems, not only curiosity but the 'home-bred charities of the heart were in it'; and the villagers, to see a Lord Mayor who had come from their own village, were allowed, at discretion, to walk between the tables of an alfresco banquet and look their hardest.

It is gratifying at this point to know that the experience of the travellers from London themselves was enlarged. The chaplain speaks again:

'The conversation at this banquet, in the intervals of the several toasts, though naturally of a desultory and general nature, was yet such as to show that good taste, good feeling and good sense are by no means limited to the citizens of the metropolis.' Beyond pointing out that the metropolis is not London but Canterbury, I can only, as an Oxford citizen, say 'How handsome of him!'

Those were days of leisure, patronage, and handsome pageant — a rather pleasant age to live in, one thinks; and it refreshes one to know that as the Barge glided from the sight of Oxford waters, 'the weather continued to be serene and beautiful; and as the vessels cleft the glassy water, they left a long, undulating track behind'.

'A City that is Compact Together'

Walk round about Zion. Tell her stones. Mark well her bulwarks.

ONCE, after a long absence in Spain and familiarity with its heavy fortress-like houses, I was astonished and a little taken aback to find that the Oxford High Street appeared by sudden contrast diminutive and even domestic. It was not for long. The curve of the High resumed its pleasure. The 'most absolute tower in England' raised its serene shelter for bells. The prospect (for it is more than a view) across the Cherwell bridge remained the most beautiful approach to Oxford and from the leads of the Camera the assured state and nobility of a University city surrounded one.

In every book on the appearance of Oxford, there are lamentations. Familiar outlines are frequently changed through building, and the unfamiliar displeases; and yet, after all, it is only Oxford as it *is* which concerns the modern observer. Most of us have never seen the bygone Oxford — and the centuries have been urbane. The pedigree of the medieval foundation upon which she was raised stiffens and straightens the lineage of her building, but above the narrow structure rises a city of a surprising gaiety of aspect. The centuries' grace and elegance are stylized like an achievement of arms. Cities of hewn stone are not common in England and the granite of Scotland does not entertain the sunlight suavely as the coloured Cotswold stone. Edinburgh, like Oxford, is a city of a fine shapes, but how its surfaces disgust the sun! In Oxford every tower and angle suns its secrets, revealing details of structure, submitting at times to shadow, but having, as it were, an understanding with the light.

Dogged survivals persist from the days of defence and fortification. The Castle Tower and the Bishop's prison in St. Michael's Tower thrust their unadorned memories of dead and gone days in Oxford history.

Now and again the city has the aspect of one of those places of pilgrimage to which multitudes of people go up. Its tides of youth flow and ebb continually — always youth, never the same youth. Long ago, no one quite knows why, youth sought this place and has never been dislodged. There have been two major migrations of the students protesting against injustice; but justice being done, they returned. Merchants and traders fled before successive visitations of the Black Death, and it was their failure to return and rebuild after the third visitation which set large spaces of derelict property at liberty for the building of Colleges. Even the fines imposed by Richard III upon those who neglected to rebuild and repair their houses did not enforce the return of the

The High from Magdalen

owners, who, having settled elsewhere, preferred to sell their liabilities. Cardinal Wolsey took astute advantage of the half-bankrupt halls and waste property to build his great college of Christ Church, setting his precedent of the confiscation of outmoded monastic buildings to be used for better purposes.

A sense of importance and dignity in setting is one of the inheritances which Oxford owes to its great ecclesiastics. Waynflete, Wykeham, Wolsey, Laud, Sheldon, all had this strong sense of a seemly and noble background for learning, and decorum in its administration. When a College became a 'seat of learning', conscious architecture arose.

Yet Oxford has no great advantage for its architectural setting. It is not far above sea-level, and its hills are not like those of Rome or Athens. A sunny and open valley inviting slow rivers is its evident amenity. Approaches from three sides look down on it and from three sides it is entered by bridges. Rome sits on seven hills. Oxford lies in its meadows. It is a city lit in the plain. It was a city to journey to. There was a bridge to pass over, gates to enter, a country ford over a quiet river.

Youth chose this place, and youth remains its living citadel and lamp. Merchants could be dislodged by plague, but youth returned to fill their room and their houses. Young men could 'throw off their gowne at the end of the Towne' and run off to join the armies at civil war but they returned.

Stone of repentance; stone of memory; stone of tragedy; stone of defence; stone of mart or use; all these are built in degree into every city that men inhabit. But seldom have they been built on so small a ground and in such impressive and noble variety.

'Turn but a stone and start a wing.'

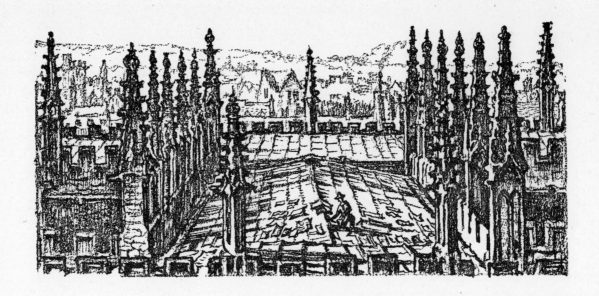

V

A Wonderful Pryer

Mr. Robert Wood told me yesterday that his uncle Anth. Wood was a wonderful pryer.
That he would go out himself in by-places, wore his hat over his eyes, seemed to take notice
of nothing and to know nothing, and yet he took notice of everything and knew everything.

A FINE for libel would seem at first sight an embarrassing possession for a Vice-Chancellor's spending; especially as the fine had to be exacted from a fellow-scholar. One could imagine that he would be at trouble to choose something discreet upon which to spend it; something as far removed from the occasion of grievance as possible! or could it be that, having a certain work in progress and being short of money, the fine of £40 upon Anthony Wood's account might appear as one of those opportune windfalls which were called at one time a godsend.

One does not know how Earl Danby's fine gate of the Physick Garden (now called Botanic Garden) would have been enriched if it had not been for Anthony Wood's (the *a* Wood is entirely his own invention) spiteful words on the Earl of Clarendon. But, his book (most woefully) burnt, his fine imposed and paid, two of the statues which still stand in the niches of Earl Danby's gate were then paid for by this misdemeanour.

What Anthony Wood thought, as he passed the decorated gateway, is not, to my knowledge, recorded. Perhaps, like the unsuccessful ticket-holders of the Irish Sweepstake, he consoled himself with the thought that after all it was for a charity. Or

12

perhaps his sardonic mind recollected that he '*could* have said a great deal more about the E. of Clarendon'.

For Anthony Wood, born at Post-Master's Hall in the Stuart times, is a slightly pathetic if very angular figure of an Oxford antiquarian and scholar during the Civil Wars; at the same time precise and unscrupulous, taciturn and slanderous, entreating affection yet making enemies everywhere.

'At the hither end of Magdalen came out of the hole behind it and the new herb-house, one Barschdale and told me I had abused his grandfather and followed muttering till I came to Magdalen College Corner. I was fain to hold up my cudgell at him.' Poor cantankerous Anthony Wood! 'Everywhere,' he complained, he was 'accused and condemned of conceitedness'; yet his diary contains this touching passage.

'Wednesday H. F. left me and I exceedingly melancholy all that day and many days following. God bless H. F.'

Soon after, the distressed Mr. Hearne (a scholar upon whom a corner of Anthony Wood's mantle fell) relates the following tale of this prickly pryer.

'I am told by one of the Fellows of Merton College that Mr. Anthony A. Wood formerly used to frequent their Common Room but that a quarrel arising one night between some of the Fellows, one of them, who thought himself very much abused, put some of the rest into Court. But when the day for deciding the matter came, there wanted sufficient evidence. At last Mr. Wood having been in company all the time the quarrel lasted, and *put down the whole in writing*, gave a full relation, which appeared so clear for the plaintiff that immediate satisfaction was commanded to be given. This was so much resented that Mr. Wood was afterwards expelled the Common Room and his company avoyded as an observing person, and not fit to be present where matters of any moment were discussed.'

It hardly sounds fair to Anthony Wood when justice seems to have been well and truly done. What the matters of moment might be from which he was to be excluded, we shall never know, but the repercussions always seemed to batter the head of the wonderful pryer whatever the dispute.

'The Society of Merton would not let me live in College for fear I should pluck it down to search after antiquities.'

The egregious Dr. Fell so altered and sub-edited his book on Oxford antiquities that he hardly recognized it and refused to have it re-published in England.

'Anthony A. Wood, as Dr. Hudson told me, consulted with him (knowing yt he had great correspondence with ye chief men in Holland) how to get his third vol of Athenae Oxon printed there. When he was asked the reason why he would not have it printed in England he answered that his other Books suffered so much by the Liberty that some men took of expunging what they pleased that he would never suffer any book of his to be committed to any English Press again. He moreover added (to use his own words) "When this volume comes out I'll make you laugh again!"'

Nevertheless, it is from this wonderful pryer with his quarrelling and collecting and erudition, that so much knowledge of Oxford and her Colleges, halls and great men descends. Everyone who has written on Oxford since his date, digs first in the quarries of Anthony Wood's great archives.

There is a pleasant story of his devotion to learning told, I am glad to say, *this* time, with the gratitude of his contemporaries. How he unearthed bundles of MSS. from Bodley's cellars, damp and mouldering and on the point of decay, and for a month nursed them back to life, taking them daily out on the leads and spreading them out to dry, turning and tending them and saving them for the Library and posterity.

But then again, alas, the reluctant Mr. Hearne, who succeeded Anthony in his work if not in his methods, has this strange story to tell of this avid and determined collector.

'Dr. Langbain has a design of enlarging Twynne's apology for ye antiq. of Oxon's and Godwin's Hist. de Praes. Angl. in order to which he had collected a heap of materials, consisting of Letters, etc.

'Mr. Thos. Tanner told Mr. Thwaites (from whom this relation comes) yt Anthony Wood told him yt upon Dr. Barrlow's promotion to ye Provostship of Queen's College he came to visit him. The Provost being then engaged, put him into a little room, where upon ye table he found three or four heaps of Paper; which, Mr. Wood consulting [the wonderful pryer] found ym to relate to the Antiquities of Oxon.

'An armful of ym he took home, covering ym with one flap of his gowne. After he had put them in his little museum of MSS. (as he calls it in his Athen. Oxon) he returned to the above-said little room whence he took ye papers. After he had staid some time there and the Provost not appearing the second time (his strangers not being gone) Wood filled his gown again with the Remains of ye sd Papers which he carried (the Boys hooting him through the street especially Logic Lane) to his own study. This done, he returns to ye Room where he waited some time and ye Provost when his strangers were gone finding him, suspected nothing of this Fraud, as not being acquainted with his sort of learning and not knowing that Dr. Langbain had any such papers.'

It sounds sadly true! The boys hooting in Logic Lane might be the report of an eye-witness, or was Anthony really so proud of this achievement that he saw no harm in relating it himself? He was certainly a Figure (if sometimes a Figure of fun) in the annals of Oxford and the Civil War, and a good deal of entertaining reading surrounds him. But it is not his hard-working and unselfish, if thorny, existence which endears him to me so much, as his happy ending. For Anthony Wood 'made a good end'.

It was not that this precise scholar was twenty-two hours a-dying; that 'God Almighty spared him so long that he had his senses entire and full time to settle all his affairs to his content', though that in itself is lovable and a wonderful death-bed for a scholar.

It is not even that he gave charge to Dr. Charlett to 'burn any loose reflecting papers' which he might find after his death. But that, antiquarian notwithstanding, *he himself had prepared for that purpose 2 bushels of them!* Now, if *I* had been capable of

Anthony Wood's House, Merton Street

collecting two bushels of loose reflecting papers, should I also have been capable of burning them even on my death-bed! Wouldn't just this or the other sharp witty reflection have seemed worth saving — 'to make you laugh again!' Not for Anthony Wood, who made this good scholar's end, easing the tension which had vexed him so much in life by this smoking out of old wasps' nests. The two bushels of the old antiquarian's venom were burnt at the stake. What a truly literal burnt-offering. It was with this liberal and happy ending, that Anthony Wood, old vinegar-bottle and pious scholar, blessed life and died.

There is a stone on the floor of Merton College Chapel which marks his resting place and a mural tablet of somewhat surprising elegance placed to his memory in the same chapel. But, cocked up on a side gable of Post-Master's Hall is a small dormer window which is that of Anthony Wood's study. Much that came and went might be observed from the half-concealed eyelet hole, and it is there that I like to fancy Oxford's 'wonderful pryer', 'taking notice of nothing, and knowing nothing, and yet seeing and knowing all'. I shall be careful of my decorum as I pass along Merton Street. Who knows, whether, glancing upward suddenly, I may find Anthony Wood observing me.

VI

'For the Year of Our Lord God'

Introit Noë in arcam Mar. 17.

ONE had heard of the Koran (or part of it) having been printed on a shroud and being once in the possession of Bodley's Librarian, but who would think at any time of that austere sheet the Oxford Almanack being printed on handkerchiefs! Since it was in the days of Anthony Wood, who mentions it, and bought some for a friend, no doubt handkerchiefs were rarer and more banner-like than they are today, when a single sheet of paper is discreetly put to the purpose of displaying in one time-saving glance, the month and day of the year of our Lord God, and the appropriate reverence of great men due for every proper occasion.

Who would have thought, either, that the clerk of Oxenford once counted time on his fingers, and that not just the tips, but the joints and knuckles as well, to adjust his ready reckoning! It is all printed in a book of the good old days with diagrams, joints, knuckles (inside *and* out) and all. Instructions as to the finding of Easter and the spacing of days of the year after the mode of Egypt and with the help of counting on fingers are all told in successive survivals of Oxford Kalendars. 'There were', says Wood, 'nearly 30,000 of them printed (1673) besides a sheet-almanack of two pence, that was then and there printed for that year; and because of the novelty of the said almanack and its title they were all vended. But the printing of it being a great hindrance to the sale of other almanacks the society of book-sellers in London, bought off the copy for the future, as only a sheet-almanack wrought off from a copper-plate was afterwards printed by the curators of Sheldon's Press.' It is the almanack and not the Kalendar (though this still survives) which flutters down the Centuries as a single sheet printed and decorated for display upon the wall. It is headed, 'For the year of our Lord God', which for some reason delights Americans. It contains curious saints not in the Church Calendar. It solemnly records Egg-Saturday. A Term ends on a liturgical antiphonal, 'O', and begins on the Feast of Saint Remigius of Rheims. There are Lucy of Syracuse, Cyprian of Antioch, Machutus of Britany, Evurtius of Orleans, St. Brituis of Tours — all hinting how closely Oxford followed the Paris model in this as in other things. But it is not so much the arrangements of days and weeks and the procession of the great and the saints in their train, which claims my attention, but rather the sequence of its decoration throughout a hundred and fifty years of its existence (1716-1865). In the beginning, the Emblematic and allegorical held supreme place; partly, it would seem, as a test of intelligence for the student. Did one complacently recognize all the inner and classical meaning of those pillars, those Olympian figures, those towers and hills? An examination paper seems to have been set in pictures for the aspirant to learning. Sometimes, so involved and numerous are the classical allusions that pamphlets were written to explain. Such a one of the date 1711 calls itself, 'An Explanation of the design of the Oxford Almanack for the year 1711, taken from the most occult Hieroglyphicks of Kircher, Pignorius, Perius, authors well-versed in all the Egyptian Learning of that kind and from several other Antient as well as modern writers.' It then proceeds with the Explanation.

A. 'The first figure represents a noble pillar of the Dorrik Order which has plainness without Rusticity; gravity without affectation, strength and stability semper eadem, and consists of the nicest Proportions that Art and nature could contrive to render it worthy the Protection of Heaven. This pillar is part of and therefore represents a Temple. This order was thought most proper by the Religious Numa for the service of the Gods, fitting for Minerva, Mars and Hercules, the Deities most conspicuous for their Virtues, being without the Gayety and Ostentation of the Fantastick Votaries, but solemn and magnificent becoming the Dignity of Man, the Decency of Matrons and void of all foreign superstitions ... Nor may this Pillar be improperly applied to the British Constitution in the State as well as Church which is grounded upon Fundamentals so just and lasting, that the Malice of its Enemies have not yet been able to overthrow it. There was no necessity to represent more than one pillar for both Church and State, they both being established upon the same foundation.'

If *all that can be made out of one single pillar*, what can one look for from 'Authors well-versed in all Egyptian Learning' with respect to the innumerable figures in classic garments scattered about the landscape of the Almanack for 1711!

It was a game which the learned played with some address. (One gathers that leisure still existed.) Dean Aldrich, who built the Peckwater Quadrangle in Christ Church, was a special adept, but I fear that neither Art nor Decoration played any part in the arrangement of his classical puzzles. There is a collection of early Almanacks before me with one 'painful' engraving of an allegory (an easy one, this!) representing the student being drawn from the enticements of pleasure and sloth to the delights of learning and science. The conductors to the realms of high thought are Minerva (very suitable) and Hercules (very necessary). The student, with, oh such pain in his expression, is no match for Hercules, though Pleasure rise from her couch to grip his withdrawing ankle and Sloth hangs to his toga. The joys of learning, i.e. the Towers of Oxford, are on a distant hill, yet the student, in spite of Hercules, is looking back.

Years ago, a young gentleman from Cambridge explained to me a system in use in his College Hall of posting the bill of fare within the doorway. There was, it seems, one delectable enticement on this official sheet of which he never knew anyone to partake. Placed last on the list, it appeared, 'Cold Vegetarian!' When I looked at the expression of the student who was being frog-marched to higher things, I suddenly 'placed' that phrase. 'Cold Vegetarian' was so obviously written on the face of that pained and shuddering student. Minerva said 'Come!' Hercules lent him a hand;

'Cold Vegetarian'! shuddered that student, turning from the remote and shining hill to the flowery earth from which he was being slowly prised.

Sometimes the piquancy of the game was heightened by the introduction of living people. That invaluable gossip Mr. Hearne detects and chronicles a bit of scandal for posterity.

'I just now saw ye Oxford Almanack for ye yeare ensuing wherein is represented the Ld Treasurer (Godolphin) playing at dice, and the Queen in a very disconsolate condition, etc., if we may believe those who are supposed to understand ye meaning.'

In the high manner we have the following:

> 'Tell us O Juno, whom thou hast sent down
> In Prophet's dress to guard the British crown.
> Is't Osborne's face or Hyde's that now appears,
> With Wisdom equal to their finished years?
> Does he not from the school of Learning come
> Known by the Muses' Hill and sacred Dome.'

But in 1723 'the famous architectural views which still at the Clarendon Press maintain their reputation were introduced as a novelty' and no one played with Allegories any more. At first the architectural composition is a mere background for the distinguished sons of the house, who hold their achievements in front of them for all to see. Dr. Paddy holds a scroll of music, Christopher Wren a scale model; Dr. Radcliffe receives the sick and halt at the door of his Infirmary. Then the romantic landscape has a period — a good period, for there was good opportunity — and then the fact that architecture apart from plan or purpose has a pictorial value of its own, steadily insisted upon itself, and there emerged the Oxford Almanack much as we have it today, for the noble views of Oxford are still unexhausted.

There were notable names among the artists' resounding disputes. Read this! 'At a time when he could not afford to pick and choose his work, Turner supplied the heading to the Official broadsheet almanac of the University of Oxford, usually a representation of the interior or exterior of some building connected with the Varsity or City. The Master of Balliol took exception to one design, the Quadrangle of the College, arguing that the play of sun-light had not been naturally rendered. On Turner refusing to humour the pedant, the design was handed over for amendment to Hugh O'Neill, a mediocre, topographical draughtsman and duly appeared under his own name. This was in 1809. Previously Turner had been requested to sketch more correctly some parts of the inside of Christ Church Hall, his artistic licence not being appreciated by the authorities, rare sticklers for photographic realism.' (*Turner, the Painter: Bernard Falk.*)

Much of this century of prints is perfunctory steel-engraving giving one nevertheless in a charming and comprehensive way the appearance of eighteenth-century Oxford, when St. Giles' was a wide grassy 'Place', where gentlemen rode their cobs and ladies in mob-caps took the air with diminutive copies of themselves beside them. The old

Passage, Old Clarendon

mill of Quaking Bridge, the Conduit in Nuneham Park; the river in all aspects, old approaches to the city and colleges — are all tried in effect. So much is there that has now gone, that turning the big pages to discover familiar buildings left unchanged becomes much the same game as that of 'classical allusions' in the early emblematic series.

Suddenly one comes upon something which has a familiar aspect. Yes! one knows them! — the time-wasted busts of the Terminals round the Sheldonian Theatre — but how handsome, how curled and refined. The tears of Oxford skies have now wasted their cheeks and moulted their beards, but I give you my word they were not always so.

In Lena Milman's life of Christopher Wren she divulges the fact that the circle of terminal figures menacing the public in front of the Sheldonian is an 'obvious adaptation of a grille of similar design in the château of Vaux-le-Vicomte of which Wren recorded his admiration in his letter from Paris'. They were meant to be grotesque she adds and 'we cannot credit Wren with all their rugged absurdity'. No, by no means![1] Mr. Wren meant them to be an added elegance. He was a young architect. This his first serious work. But the Almanack shows these reigning beauties as anything but grotesque — curls all in place — noses correct, the English vine — (the hop-leaf and its blossoms) — all arranged in their hair for a party. I am on the side of the Almanack in its testimony to beauty. No Mr. Mantalini could be more elegant than Mr. Wren's male choir.

It is always puzzling to know why certain Saints survive in importance and not others. Why St. Swithin and not St. Valentine? St. Scholastica's Day was important because (incredible though it sounds) until the year 1825 Mayor and Aldermen and City Councillors of Oxford did penance in St. Mary's Church for the murder of four undergraduates on that day by the townspeople in the reign of King John. Egg-Saturday (*Festum Ovorum* in the Almanack) must have been of great importance to a rather scrabbling collection of medieval boys. 'O Sapientia' are the opening words of the last of an octave of antiphonals to the Magnificat which were sung in October, all of which began with 'O'. Thus on the day on which 'O Sapientia' was sung in church, the October Term came to an end.

Certain things *do* become lodged in people's minds in some way. Never, for instance, even in the year 1505 can I believe that the record on the Kalendar 'Introit Noë in Arcam Mar. 17th' was of great spiritual succour to the Oxford clerk or to anybody else. It is true that the story is completed by the later record '*Exit* Noë ab arca', but has it really taken us any further?[2]

[1] The busts as they stand are not those originally placed in position by Wren. The latter were considered in 1868 to be worn-out or unsafe and the present busts were substituted. The displaced busts which, one supposes, Wren supervised himself, are some of them to be found in College gardens; one or two, I believe, in private grounds. The material used is better in quality and there is every indication that dignity and ornament were sought. It is difficult to imagine Wren 'passing' such figures as those brooding on their wrongs in the Broad St. circle. Perhaps the original weather-beaten busts *did* give some later mason the idea of the grotesque. But Wren had no such purpose in the decoration of his serious and noble building.

[2] From the *Manchester Guardian* of March 17th, 1950, I learn that this date, now St. Patrick's Day, was long ago celebrated as 'the anniversary of the entry of Noah into the ark and a very popular festival, marked by the staging of morality plays about the Flood, and much buffoonery and jollification'.

VII

Oxford's 'Repository of Rarities'

Not learned but very industrious. (John Evelyn of Elias Ashmole.)

EVERYTHING, it is well known, must have a beginning and the beginning of Oxford's Repository of Rarities, the earliest science museum in England, was in *Tradescant's Ark* in Lambeth. This, in its turn, began because the Tradescants (father and son) were botanists and gardeners and were sent by noble patrons and employers to foreign places (Muscovy, Barbary, The Aegean Islands) in search of new plants and trees to acclimatize in England.

Botanists have a pretty way of leaving their traces in the country. Flowers and plants perpetuate their discoveries, and *tradescantia* blooms happily in gardens which never heard of the Tradescants. The rarities which these famous gardeners collected were additional to their real research into plants, and of secondary interest to them. Their great concern was the arranging of a complete physick garden in Lambeth. The 'Ark' was a diversion, named so by some wit because it housed numbers of Zoological specimens. Everyone who has returned from foreign parts with trophies of flamboyant pottery, shawls, beads and baskets, knows ruefully how seldom these things, so gay in their own country, fit into rooms of an English house, and how sooner or later a cupboard with a glass door is introduced to isolate the 'curios'. What, for instance, could poor Mrs. Tradescant do with her husband's collection of boots?

'The King's Great Porter's boots.

'Little Jeffrey's boots.

20

'Boots from Lapland, Greenland, Muscovy, Babylonia, Russia and Persia.

'Shoes to walk on snow without sinking.

'Shoes from Peru, Canada, Mogull, China, Japan, Coromandell, Barbary, Turkey, Venise, Rhode, Malta, Poland, Greenland, Portugall, Spaine, Russia (shod with iron) East Indies.

'Sandalls of wood from China. Sandalls made of twigs and several sorts of sandalls from Venise, Malta, etc.'

What could she do with the Dodo? A Museum was indicated: and the 'Ark' of the Tradescants became a favourite resort of the curious and the enlightened. Noblemen who came to see the plants and the garden stayed to visit the Ark. It became a pet plaything for the gentlemen of the period, who added to it rarities on their own account. Charles II himself appears as a donor[1] and when the collection was moved to Oxford his cipher was placed above the door (now a window).

The Tradescants also had a neighbour in Lambeth, a certain Elias Ashmole (not, I fear, a favourite with Mrs. Tradescant), and to this neighbour, himself a busy collector, the younger Tradescant bequeathed the contents of the famous Ark. It was all too much for poor Mrs. Tradescant, who either set too high a value upon the contents of the Ark, or too low an estimate on Mr. Elias Ashmole, for she refused, with slanderous accusations, to allow him to remove his legacy from her house and finally, after solemnly recanting and confessing her slanders before a magistrate, drowned herself in a pond.

In this manner Mr. Ashmole acquired the Ark with its inhabitants and rarities. The Tradescants had been educated collectors. 'It is well worthy of remark that in the whole of the catalogue not a single monstrosity is named.' Siege-money interested them and the collecting of coins was as ardent a pursuit in those days as the writing of diaries. The collection of exotic woods, of gums and earths for dyeing was in their own line of research, but the 430 birds, reptiles and insects, and all save the feet and beak of the Dodo from Mauritius, went the way of dissolution down which crawled the crocodiles of the physicians' laboratories.

'I believe not learned, but very industrious,' said Mr. Evelyn of Elias Ashmole. He was not a traveller himself. His precursor in the Curious, Mr. Coryat of the 'Crudities', walked from Venice to the northern seaboard of France and hung his shoes up in his parish church of Odcombe at the end of it. But Elias himself was full of the small ailments of the sedentary man and a most restless curiosity. One wonders what the man will be up to next.

'I began to learn to dissect a body.'

'About this time I began to learn Hebrew of Rabbi Solomon Frank.' 'Having entered upon the study of plants, this day about three o'clock was the first time I went simpling.'

[1] Inscription on exhibition ticket under model of a warship in Ashmolean Museum: 'English Warship about 1634. This vessel, the earliest known English ship-model, may be the toy given by Phineas Pett to Charles II when a boy.'

'I Christened Mr. Fox his son at Oxford 4 p.m.

'Mr. Henry Hinde, organist of the Cathedral, taught me the Virginall and the organ.'

'In this year I was taught the harpsichord by Mr. Farmiloe.'

'I was admitted to Clement's Inn. —I was entered a gentleman of the Ordnance.'

'About this time I began to learn seal-graving, casting in sand and goldsmith's work.'

He seems to have had almost as many marriages as occupations, each one a little more advantageous than the former, and his credulities were even more numerous. I often wonder how he contrived to hang his spiders round his neck to cure his ague! Cortés had an emerald jewel to contain his scorpion, but Mr. Ashmole? Pepys had no patience with his astrology and nonsense.

The Civil War had been a time of great disruption and destroying, and it is hardly to be wondered at that men began to find pleasure in preserving and in building up. Perhaps that fact also explains the frequent diaries of the period. Oxford had begun to be the repository of other things besides rarities. The Arundel and Pomfret marbles had come to settle there and the University showed an extraordinary complaisance in building a Repository to house Elias Ashmole's collection of rarities (1683).[1] The expense cannot have been slight, for the 'Old Ashmolean' as it is now called, is of a high type of architecture. An old print of the building gives the name of the architect as T. Wood, but Belcher and Macartney (*Later Renaissance in England*) 'consider this by no means conclusive, deciding, however, that there is apparent in the building the work of two men, and that the fine doorway may be placed to Wren's credit'. It is quite good enough for Wren and an early print of the museum before the new buildings of Exeter shouldered it into the background, shows it to be so good as to march with Wren's Sheldonian Theatre in perfect propriety — the first museum opened in England. Recalling the great battle over the building of the Science Museum in Oxford, one sees how easy-going was the mentality of the University of that day, which could afford, and had the inclination, to build such a handsome building for the purpose of housing the contents of Tradescant's Ark and Elias Ashmole's books and papers. No one ever called the Ashmole Museum the 'Cockatrice Den' as they later did the Science Museum. King Charles deputed the Duke of Gloucester to open the building and all the celebrities in Oxford came to see it done. For Ashmole collected, if not the very greatest, at any rate sufficiently famous men about him as he collected rarities. He held official positions. He catalogued Royal Collections. He was one of the first Freemasons, and his great work on the History of the Garter (thirty-nine volumes) was housed in the Museum. I think we may safely agree with Mr. Evelyn that, though not learned, Elias Ashmole was decidedly industrious; and it is to this busybody of learning that we owe the founding of the first Museum of Natural History in Britain.

[1] The plan was also to include a School of Natural History and a chemical Laboratory.

Degree Day

Portraits of Mr. Ashmole and the Tradescants now hang in the 'Founder's Room' of the new Ashmolean Gallery, looking down on the remnants of the rarities gathered there by the bequest of the latter and the persistence of the former. The gems lying on the table in the portrait of Ashmole can be identified in the Museum. Like Pepys, Ashmole kept a diary in cypher which is now being deciphered. But all the scandalous matter which has up to the present titillated the public is that the frame of Mr. Ashmole's own portrait was carved by Grinling Gibbons himself!

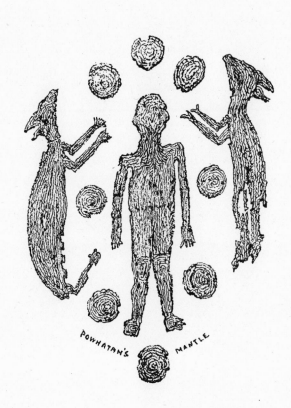

VIII

Patios and Pinnacles

I will build such a thing in the sky.   MICHELANGELO
*The assemblage of buildings in that quarter, [Radcliffe Square] though no single one is beautiful,
always struck me with singular pleasure, as it conveys such a vision of large edifices unbroken by
private houses, as the mind is apt to entertain of renowned cities that exist no longer.*
                                                                                    H. WALPOLE

THERE was a time, not long ago, when the daring undergraduate climbed to forbidden roofs and monuments and left a token there as a sign of his excursion into disobedience. But the war took the wind somewhat out of his sails, for not only was he allowed on such unlikely heights, but he was encouraged to go there — nay! even ordered and stationed there. Ladders were the only wear for Oxford College roofs in those latter days, and night-watching the honourable sport. Travellers through the air in this Year of Grace must see as strange sights as any Fynes Morrison Wonder. You hover above a Gothic and Eastern city; a city of square patios and pinnacled leads, with squat dividing trees. From the top of the Campanile in Venice it once surprised me to find that the canals, such a feature of the city beneath, were invisible. A huddle of roof-tops beside the sea was the famous city of Venice. But Oxford from the air is as surprisingly extended, displayed like a series of battlemented galleries, each hoarding a shadow and a garden, a labyrinth of high ramparts, lying foursquare. Undergraduate, College servant, Don, have climbed there and patrolled, to watch the heavens with the attention of an Eastern shepherd; not for the wheeling of the constellations to space the watch, but for the rushing of dark wings to blot the stars.

Once in every century, the Fellows of All Souls remember their origin, and pace the leads of their College singing a foolhardy chant upon some illusory bird called the Mallard. The words, laid up in lavender from century to century, must recall to them the extravagances of their youth. But it was no illusory bird which was watched on the roofs of Oxford, but the brooding of mortal hate. The fireball and not the mallard was hunted in those fantastic and eerie nights of the moon. Pockets for lodging danger were crowded on the gables. Such knowledge of college roofs and parapets has never been known before.

Once I saw the roofs of the city leading like a great stair to the Dome of the Camera, which dominates, as every great dome will, the famous towers and spires. There is an advantage in living on a northern slope above the city. One never sees it in shadow. It is always lit, and the caprices or caresses of the sunlight are as manifold as the coming

Radcliffe Camera and All Souls

of morning and evening. It is a city of a heavenly silhouette against shadowy slopes and refining mists.

In a winter of snow I watched the roofs of Oxford transformed as if the city had been rebuilt in the night. Snow, which often etherealizes a landscape, had laid a solid stairway on the roofs of Oxford, white treads leading up to and supporting, as it seemed, an unfamiliar filigree Dome. The houses beneath the blanched planes were shadows. The only shining surfaces, unobscured, led step by step to the Dome, lying splendid and compact beneath the sunlit and contracted winter sky. The stairway vanished at noon and with it the ascent of one of those 'Renowned cities that exist no longer', a stairway in a Château d'Espagne.

IX

'Moun Bien Mondain'

Oxford — August 29th, 1806.
Borrowed this day of the Rev. the Bodleian Librarian, the picture given to the Library by Mr.
Peters which I promise to return on demand.

JOSEPH WHITE

Mem. Not returned   June 24th, 1807.
Nor as yet   October, 1808.
And never to be returned (added at a later date).

EVERY now and then pictorial incidents will happen in an Oxford thoroughfare with as little disturbance as though they arose from the street like a fountain and would probably subside there again.

If, for instance, you were walking on a certain empty Sunday morning down the High Street, you might be astonished to see four men in the uniform of heralds blowing a fanfare on silver trumpets outside the porch of St. Mary-the-Virgin. You would thereby understand that the Judge of Assize is going to church.

He will sit, his approving clever face interested and attentive, and hear a Latin sermon. The congregation will sing Latin hymns and listen to a most resounding telling-over of names, ringing like chimes on a dulcimer, of benefactors to the University for centuries past, for whom, in this special and impressive manner the University yearly gives thanks to God.

It is a sonorous tale of names[1] which God and the congregation hear. Founders of Colleges, Pious women, Archbishops and Lawgivers, Kings and noblemen, Givers of land, Givers of money, Givers of books — Fine generosity of noble donors, remembered in many cases in this one Bidding Prayer and a shadowed tablet in a cloister, or the still more shadowy catacombs of Bodley's cellars.

Very early in the list, and most romantic of all the imposing names, sounds that of Humphrey Duke of Gloucester, who brought the new learning of Italy to England and fostered it there, lover of the Italian Renaissance, of splendid buildings and noble books, and who founded and built the magnificent library still called by his name. He died in 1447.

Some hundreds of years later than the royal (but tragic and dissolute) figure of England's Renaissance Prince, lived the devoted and somewhat acidulated Jacobite

[1] *Bodleian Library: Album Benefactorum.* The Registrar of Benefactors was begun in 1600 under the personal care of Sir Thomas Bodley. The Latin Statutes of 1610 provide that it shall be kept up to date and always exposed to view, both as a mark of gratitude to benefactors and as an encouragement to others who may be ready to follow them.

Entrance, Old Bodleian

scholar called Mr. Hearne, who, in his own words, 'Whenever he saw the Duke Humphrey's signature on a volume was accustomed to pay it a mark of special respect' (surmised a kiss). From him also comes the information that it was the custom of Duke Humphrey to write in his own books the motto 'Moun bien mondain' (my worldly good).

But as no book of Duke Humphrey has been recovered bearing this legend, and several belonging to his private physician Dr. Gilbert Kymer, Vice-Chancellor of the University, are thus inscribed, the legend seems to be now among those 'facts' which ought to be true if they aren't. For no sounder motto could have been invented for this impassioned lover of books or have better displayed the importance with which he regarded them.

It was the actual making and increase of books for his own pleasure which he first fostered, sending to Italy and commissioning scribes to copy books of the humanistic learning at great cost to his private purse. ('Books', needless to say, were in those days manuscript, and often unique.) The collector's joy succeeded, and Duke Humphrey began to acquire a library. Books in their turn attract books, and Duke Humphrey began to be a magnet for any rare and unusual authors. 'To no other men of his time were such gifts in such profusion given.'

Donors of books to the University have always been prettily thanked. There must have been a *genre* of letter-writing, both begging and thanking. It needs practice to be so adroit as this:—

'To Mr. Thomas Knolle, Citizen of London. Grocer. 1443.

'We hear that you regard our University with favour and propose to give us a copy of Josephus' Antiquities! This is a happy thought, for we possess not the book; and now instead of being in private hands and holden under a bushel, it will be raised aloft to give light to all in the household of God. Doubtless the beatific vision will be the reward of those whose actions have strengthened the faith, and in the meantime we shall pray for your welfare here and hereafter.'

Or still more this. — To Edmund Reed, Esq., 1453.

'We are sure that, when you gave us timber for the building of the new school of theology, your intention was to complete the work; for true praise is for him not who begins but who completes that he has begun. Will you then graciously give us some stone which we now sorely need. . . .'

If only Oliver Twist had had the knack!

Looking at the list of books which Duke Humphrey presented to the University of Oxford one notices first the large number of Italian authors — Boccaccio — Petrarch — Dante. The usual order for such catalogues is followed — The Bible — theological works — medicine — astronomy and mathematics — law — and in Humphrey's case this large preponderance of classic and Italian authors.

In these days of sixpenny classics only a languid enthusiasm is now available for the possession of extraordinary books. One has even lived to hear Mr. Bernard Shaw write heatedly to the papers against the purchase of the unique *Codex Sinaiticus* — saying that a facsimile copy will do just as well. But in the days when books could be taken as valuable pledges, when special statutes regulated their borrowing, and University stationers were appointed to assess them and see that no volume was traded outside the city and so lost to the University, books were treasured and chained. The spread of printing cheapened eventually the regard with which they were held, but that was after many years. The scribe and the illuminator were in Duke Humphrey's day the only producers of books.

There had been isolated attempts to collect a University Library before the time of Duke Humphrey — of that of the monks of Durham only a solitary reference is now existing, but the Bishop of Worcester, Thos. Cobham, did actually (1327) bequeath sufficient books to the University to have a chaplain appointed to look after them. Isolated bequests of a few books are not infrequent and these were either chained in the chancels of churches or left in chests in the room over the Congregation House at St. Mary's Church.

The books given by Duke Humphrey were also first kept in chests, one bearing the Arabian Nights' name of 'The chest of the three philosophies and the seven sciences.'

When you borrowed a book you deposited a pledge equivalent in value and said an *Ave* and *Pater Noster* for the repose of the soul of the benefactor. Not all books were returned, a student sometimes finding the book he had borrowed of more value to him than the pledge he had deposited, and when books were actually recovered with the name of Duke Humphrey imperfectly erased, one manner of the disposal of his books becomes apparent. King Edward's Visitors did much to complete the desolation.

For there was but a shell left of Duke Humphrey's library when Thomas Bodley in 1598 became 'thoroughly persuaded that in my solitude and surcease from commonwealth affairs, I could not busie myself to better purpose than by redusing that place (which then in every part lay ruined and waste) to the publique use of students'.

For books, though potent, are defenceless; and also, when there is only one copy which everyone uses, they wear out.

Not all 'books' were bound, and stitched sheets can be quickly separated. There are sad tales to be told of them in Oxford as elsewhere — of Abbots trading in books for kitchen comforts; of 'heretics' tearing up and destroying; of theft; of borrowing and not returning; of neglect (as later Bodley's own Library was threatened by the looting of the uneducated Cavalier soldiers until protection came by way of Fairfax the Puritan general). Whatever the causes, and the printing of books had already belittled the value of the MS. both by novelty and numbers, the shell lay despoiled and empty, and it was Bodley's ambition to refurnish it in the grand manner of Duke Humphrey. 'I hope for the beame you will take such a course as there shall be no want of beauty or strenth to the walle, which are the verie maine and principal pointes that I aim at in my building.'

Duke Humphrey's Library

No arrangements should take from the building's beauty and magnificence. So insistent was Bodley that the Library should be a fine work of art that only folios and quartos might be kept on its shelves and these must be chained. The smaller and un-bound books were to be guarded in chests and cupboards.

Again, as in Duke Humphrey's days, books attracted books, gift suggested gift, until there was the triumphant judgment: 'The books that are contained within this Librarie are verie rare strange or scarce; seldome or not at all to be heard of or seene in any place but there. All of them verie richly gilded and many of them bossed either with silver or golde.'

To the new Library came the Earl of Essex's loot from the libraries of Cadiz, for which 'he received the University's gratulatory letter for books given to the publicke library 1598'.

To Bodley's Library came the gifts of the Earl of Pembroke and of Cromwell. 'After the death of Sir Thomas Bodley, the Earl of Pembroke, by the persuasion of Archbishop Laud, gave to the Library all the collection of Greek MSS. which Francis Baroccio the Venetian had collected with great pains and cost and which is thought to be the most valuable that ever came into England at one time. The Earl reserved twenty-two of them for his own use, but these were afterwards bought and presented to the Library by Oliver Cromwell.' Gower's *Confessio Amantis* was also presented by Cromwell. Sir Kenelm Digby presented 200 Oriental MSS. — and so it goes on.

It may have been the fate of Duke Humphrey's collection which caused Bodley to formulate his strict rule about the lending of books, for not even King Charles, or later Cromwell, could have the rule relaxed. Both of them perforce commended the integrity of Bodley's librarian, but I fancy both were a trifle nettled at the refusal to lend outside the building. Also, it is another sad tale about books that the 'enemy of the librarian is the reader'. So read *inside* at the Bodleian you *must* or not read at all; and though it is under excessive vigilance that you read, it is still an exalted experience to study in Duke Humphrey's Library.

You inherit learning and the arts in a rich setting to begin with. Though the present room was extensively restored, it is such as Duke Humphrey of the Renaissance would have admired, for once settled admirably in time and a building becomes timeless. There is quiet in its arrangement and beauty in its colour and gilding. The system of shelving which was usual in D. Humphrey's day is used, making for each reader a privacy and a quiet 'carrel'.

It may be that if I were a Portuguese student wearing a cloak which, like a Spanish lady's fan, does everything but talk, I could study with profit in the baroque magnificence of the Library of Coimbra. But being of the tender-eyed races of the North, with a mind for seclusion, I reach the narrow stall in Duke Humphrey's Library, lighted by the golden light of old silver-stain glass-workers, with the happy peace of a sail dropping in harbour. This narrow light is the best possible company for a reader, just at one's elbow and setting a cautionary heaven between oneself and the garden outside.

The old clergyman who has gradually erected a barricade of books between himself and the next student, may dream in peace with a sky of pure gold beside him. If his eye wanders, it is only to the pleasant imaginings of other, it may be, more decorative minds.

There are only three books of Duke Humphrey's there now. If Mr. Hearne wished to show his 'particular mark of respect' to the signature of that 'most learned and pious prince', he would have to go on a respectful pilgrimage to many and scattered Libraries, even to France. But for a reader to climb the easy stair, obedient finger on lip, be free of that nice enclosure with its gentle gradations of silence and light, is to inherit in no small spiritual measure the *bien mondain* of Duke Humphrey.

It is something of a delight too, to discover that the most important doorway in the University of Oxford is also its lowliest. There is nothing to guide a stranger to it — only a door in a dim corner of a courtyard, leading to an old wooden stair. 'Silence!' That is required of one, but for what purpose no one discloses. It is a very humble door which leads to so much grandeur.

The High from Queen's

X

The Golden Streets

NOVEMBER is not the month of happy reputation in the English year and climate. To most ears, the very intonation 'hath a dying fall'. And yet early November, when the streets of Oxford are filled with the dual gold of a low, hovering sunlight and the transparency of shining mellow leaves, is the very season when the City is most beautiful, and when, by a paradox, its antiquity glows with youth.

The streets have ceased to be the heat-weary flags of Summer. The sunlight lays no sombre mats of shadow upon them. The core of coolness in the day soothes one's haste to withdraw into the shade. The uneasy weight of Summer has been raised and the subtlety of Autumn advances in the streets. No one quite detects the moment when the delicate apparition enters. The early morning has a new quality, like a bead of snow within a goblet of amber wine. Vigour is quickened. But the pouring of quiet gold is for the eyes and the mind. Some quality as old as the sunshine emerges from the stone — a warmth not only of this year but of centuries of years — and marries with the light, and the very fabric of the buildings seems illuminated by its own shining. No newer building ever acquires this radiance. No trees of younger growth can vaunt this gentle gold which covers the gardens and towers of Oxford with a heavenly stain. It is as if yearly the City in age assumes, and that with happy graciousness, the kind of rich apparel with which the young love to array themselves for a solemnity, a mantle of sober gold.

31

XI

'The Stone Shall Cry out of the Wall'

I can find no remedy against this consumption of the purse. Borrowing but lingers it out again and again.   FALSTAFF

To one side of the Earl Danby's fine entrance to the Botanic Garden can be seen two inscriptions in the wall. One, in English, marks the site of the Jewish burial ground in Oxford until the year 1290, in which year all Jews were expelled from England. The other, in Hebrew character,[1] is set as a memorial to those Jews who were buried there centuries ago. In the curious Eastern manner, the short passages of scripture which commemorate the dead in this second inscription are arranged to conceal a cryptogram of the date of the year of the expulsion. The shadowed exterior even now holds the gravity of a burial-ground, as the sunny interior its peace, though centuries have passed since the last Jew slept on his couch.

These inscriptions, with two other memorial stones, were placed ceremonially in position in 1931 in honour of Dr. Neubauer of the Bodleian, by the Jewish Historical Society 'in presence of the Vice-Chancellor of the University, the Mayor of Oxford, and a large gathering of people'.

A second stone, on the face of the present town hall (itself the traditional site of a religious house — *domus conversorum*[2] — for Jewish converts to the Christian Faith) contains merely a statement of fact, defining the boundary of the ancient Jewry within the city of Oxford, a settlement so close to the Priory of St. Frideswide and its activities, that like opposing currents the tides of fanaticism rose to turbulence and an old stone erected by the Jews of Oxford, but this time under compulsion and as punishment, had to be raised. Though long mutilated and buried, the shaft and base

---

[1] The letters of the Hebrew alphabet are also (as in that of the Roman) the numerals. In the inscription certain letters are marked with a small arrow and it is these letters, taken in their numerical value, which compose the date of the cryptogram. Four short passages of Scripture, chosen carefully to include the required letters, form, with slight alterations, a sequence. The passages occur in:

Habbakuk ii, 4. 'The stone shall cry out of the wall.'

Genesis xxxv, 20. 'The same is the memorial on Rachel's grave.' [The word Israel has been substituted for Rachel.]

Isaiah lvii, 2. 'He entereth into peace. They rest in their beds.'

Daniel xii, 2. ['And many of them that sleep in the dust of the earth shall awake] some to everlasting life.'

In brackets at the end of the inscription are the dates 4937-5050, dates of the Jewish Calendar corresponding to 1177-1290 Anno Domini.

[2] It is now supposed that no *domus conversorum* existed in Oxford, though the tradition is old and persistent.

of a stone cross, probably that set up by Oxford Jews as expiation for an insult by one of their number to the processional crucifix of the Priory in the year 1268, was uncovered during alterations to the President's house at Corpus, for the cross had been placed in the street near Merton College, 'and it was on the spot where it is most likely the cross was erected that this relic was found, for the old road past Merton is under the site of part of the President's garden'. (*Oxford's College Gardens: E. Sinclair Rohde.*)

The third memorial, hidden away in the only remaining part of Osney Abbey which is still standing — a small outbuilding probably once used as a store — commemorates the death by burning of Robert of Reading, a Christian deacon, who became a Jewish proselyte, taking the name of Haggai of Oxford, and who was degraded from his Christian office by the Council of Oxford (1222) and summarily burnt outside the abbey premises.   The inscription reads:

Near this stone, in Osney Abbey,
Robert of Reading,
otherwise Haggai of Oxford,
suffered for his faith,
on Sunday 17th April 1222 A.D.
Corresponding to 41 YYAR 4982 A.M.

The various stones punctuate in a curious way the passage of the Jews through Oxford in the Middle Ages, and emphasize the difficulties which arose both for them and for others because of the 'separateness' of the race, a 'separateness' as much of their own seeking as of that imposed upon them.

They came, French-speaking, with the Normans from France, but as the fusion between the conquerors and the native race gradually took place, this particular race of 'foreigners' remained persistently apart, living closely together, sharing no worship, refusing to eat with their neighbours and observing alien rites and other holy days. 'Foreigners' were in any case looked upon with suspicion and these people remained so very foreign. Dr. Neubauer does not think that the pre-expulsion Jews in Oxford left any mark upon the University of learning generally.   They came (presumably from Wallingford) to do business with the merchants and tradesmen in the thriving market town, for at that time Oxford was pre-eminently a city of tradesmen, the students hanging on as best they might. 'We never hear', says Mr. Salter, 'of a cow or sheep that was housed in Oxford, there was no mixed population of tradesmen and farmers. Oxford was solely a collection of tradesmen.' Dealers in money invariably follow prosperous trading, and the Jews, who had the monopoly of the banking trade, became important and active in the comfortable market-town.   They were never expelled from Oxford as they were from Cambridge and other towns, though many must have fled before the anger of the students in the year 1243. Their history in Oxford as elsewhere in England before their expulsion, was what might be expected of an alien people, living in the country without any status as citizens, but solely as 'chattels' of the King. 'Quia ipsi Judaei et omnia sua regis sunt.' The advantage to the Jew of this arrangement (not of his own seeking) was that he could be punished for misdemeanour or crime by no one but the King and the King was only one man and not a multitude. The advantage to the King was, that if no one but he himself might exact fines from the Jews for their offences, a happy arrangement for the royal treasury might result.

'The King (Henry III) having again wasted all his money on that swarm of foreigners whom he still kept about him, caused a rumour to be spread of some sudden invasion from Spain. Whereupon the Parliament was summoned in all haste and great sums demanded for the defence of the kingdom. But the Barons, seeing through his design, told him plainly they believed nothing of the story. As soon as there was any likelihood of war, they would provide all things necessary for it, but for the present did not care to divide their substance with foreigners. The King, therefore, parting from them in a hurry, commissioned his brother Earl Richard to raise what money he wanted upon the Jews.' (*Tovey*.)

Political bad feeling could be very easily fomented under such circumstances, and the Jews (who had no choice but to give to the King) came to be regarded as enemies of the people. Under eschatalogical penalties, and 'by warrant of scripture' the Church forbade any baptized person to traffic in usury. The Jews were the only money-lenders and with their fatal ability they applied themselves to the only profession allowed to them.

There is a curious fallacy, rather wide-spread, that a borrower of money is an innocent and hapless person, while a lender is a shark, a harpy, a 'Jew'. From the Foolish Virgins downwards, the improvident person would exploit the forethought of the provident. But if you are one of these believers, try the experiment of lending money to a hardened borrower and then trying to get it back again! Some twinge of sympathy for the usurer will surely visit you! Yet the Jews, living exempt from local taxation, taking no civic responsibility, withdrawn always into one quarter of the town and contributing nothing to its advancement, subject to no punishment from the law, but only by caprice of the King, cared little for their fellow subjects and less for the clerks of Oxford. If they had hoped, which is very unlikely, to make money out of needy students, they would have been quickly undeceived, though there came a time when the King had to set a limit to the amount of interest they might charge to the students of the University.

As the King's 'Serfs' the Jews drew further and further apart from the ordinary citizens, setting their own prohibitions against intermingling and intermarriage with Christians and bent on preserving the 'Race' from deterioration. Long before the Christian era, the cry of Race has disturbed the Jews. At the beginning of their history it was their incentive to cruel and remorseless conquest and to relentless purges of their own people. Later, when conquest and captivity fell upon themselves, it became the dynamic of a dispersed and driven people. That every nation should bring its tribute to Zion; that the Kings of the earth should bow down at her feet, makes heady and

Old Gateway, Botanic Gardens

dangerous teaching, and spiritual arrogance has often betrayed sons of their race. It was presumably such an overweening moment which caused the Jewish fanatic to rush from the crowd watching the procession on St. Frideswide's Day and, seizing the silver processional crucifix, throw it to the ground and trample upon it; and it is significant of the influential position of the Jews in the city that neither Church nor citizens might exact restitution either for the damaged property or what would certainly be regarded as the gravest sacrilege. Nor was the King's delayed punishment severe. The silver crucifix was replaced at the expense of the Jews and the erection and maintenance of the stone cross in Merton Street imposed. But resentment smouldered among the Oxford people. Arrogance is always a short-sighted attitude of mind and the Jewish population of England, claiming the protection of the King as his serfs, forgot that Kings may die and that successors may be of another mind towards them. Edward I was not Henry III or John, and he was awake to other aspects of the Jewish settlement in England ignored by his fore-runners. After the imposing of restrictions on their movements, the banning of usury to their people, the curtailment of privilege, it was by the King's decree and that only, that the Jews were banished from England.

It is many years since the Rabbis decided against the admission of proselytes to the Jewish synagogue; so long, in fact, that such a thing seems now unthinkable. But when the Jews were prosperous before the expulsion, their leaders were active enough, and proselytes increased. It was to counteract this movement that the Dominicans came to settle in Oxford and it is of this time that the stone set up in Osney speaks with retrospective eloquence. The story of Robert of Reading is probably familiar. The legal aspect of his trial, 'The first trial before an ecclesiastical court for heresy in England', is discussed by Professor F. W. Maitland in his book 'Roman Canon Law in the Church of England', an essay which was reprinted by the Jewish Historical Society.

A certain deacon of the Church, Robert of Reading, having fallen in love with a Jewess called Matilda, who stipulated that if she married him he must become a Jew, submitted to the rite of circumcision and took the name of Haggai of Oxford in the year 1222. In the same year, in the Abbey of Osney, the new Archbishop of Canterbury, Stephen Langton, back from the Lateran Council in Rome, called a Council in the Abbey known as the Council of Oxford. It was before this council that the apostate deacon was summoned and degraded. No sentence otherwise seems to have been passed upon him by the Council. 'He was degraded by the Lord of Canterbury outside the Church and before the people.' (*Walter of Coventry.*) 'He was burnt with fire outside the town by the King's bailliffs who were present on the spot.' (*Ann. Monast.*) 'When he had been degraded he was burnt by the servants of the Lord Fawkes, Sherriff of Oxford.' (*Ralph of Coggeshall.*) So much of fact emerges from the legends which are gathered about the story. Even the chronicles of Osney Abbey, where one might expect to find detail, give only bald facts, though they add that the deacon had profaned the Host which was afterwards discovered incorrupt and unsullied.

It has been suggested that Robert of Reading was a 'Converso' or a Jewish convert to Christianity, who under strong feeling lapsed to his original faith. It is interesting, though I have found no evidence for this, for the Conversos ('Marranos' as they were called in Spain and Portugal) became an increasingly acute problem in any country where they were found in numbers, and laws against them grew increasingly severe. On the face of it a Converso was simply a Jewish convert to Christianity, but in practice, great numbers professed conversion for their own security or business standing, conforming to Catholic requirements in public, while privately following their own rites and profession as Jews. This duplicity had in the end a fatal reaction, and a Converso became very much a suspected person, his position being often of great peril.

The Jews had not been entirely absent from England[1] during the three centuries following their expulsion. Jewish Converts to Christianity had been admitted from time to time. Queen Elizabeth had a Jewish physician. There were certainly numbers of professed converts living in London under the Catholic mask, whose status was irregular and it was to discuss the readmission of the Jews to England and the regularizing of their position if they came, that Cromwell summoned a representative conference in London in the year 1655. To this conference the President of Magdalen and a Canon of Christ Church went, as representatives of the University. There had been various attempts on the part of the Jews during the three hundred years of their exile to return to England, as one country after another closed its privileges to them, but no one wanted displaced persons in quantities then, any more than they have done since. It is at this point of Cromwell's rule in the year 1655 that Rembrandt's genial and learned Rabbi, Menasseh ben Israel, walks out of his frame and lives for us. Of a family of Jews exiled from Portugal and living in Amsterdam, Menasseh ben Israel was visited by the ancient Jewish dream, this time in its more humanizing aspect. He came, by permission of the Protector, to England, an ambassador for the readmission of the Jews into England once more. Cromwell was sympathetic and called his conference in London. There appeared to be no legal reason why the Jews should not return, for they had not been amenable to the laws, but only to the King, and the motion which Cromwell brought before his conference was duly tabled — 'That the Jews deserving it, may be admitted into this nation, to trade and traffic and dwell amongst us as Provi-

[1] The following quotation from Dr. Neubauer throws some light on this point.

'It is probable that a great number of Jews remained in England after the Expulsion, protected by monastic authorities as converted Jews. It is most likely that they followed secretly, like the Maranos, their brethren in Spain, the Jewish rites. It may be also that the Jewish refugees from Spain in 1490 found an asylum in England. Indeed, the Spanish Ambassador complained about it to Henry VII when he was negotiating the marriage of his son Arthur with Katherine of Aragon. Certain it is that early in the fifteenth century, Jews settled in London without much molestation. But out of London (says Mr. Lee) the earliest definite trace of Jews in England is found in Oxford under Elizabeth and James. The two Universities of Oxford and Cambridge possessed at all times wide privileges of asylum. In 1608 two Jews who were not members of the University were allowed to read in the Bodleian. Alexandro Armidi, a Florentine, taught Hebrew at Oxford, also a convert. In 1650 a Jew opened a coffee-house at Oxford; and Isaac Abendana occurs in the accounts of Madgalen College as receiving in 1691 £2 for teaching Hebrew in the College. He edited the Oxford Almanack 1692-1700 and resided in Oxford.' (*The Jews in Oxford: Neubauer.*)

dence shall give occasion.' But the noble and disarming appeal of Cromwell — 'Bear with men of different minds from yourselves' — the candour and hope of the conference, in which Dr. Goodwin, President of Magdalen, and Henry Williamson, Canon of Christ Church, took active part and where 'The moderate majority, impressed probably by a weighty and elaborate opinion drawn up by Dr. Barlow, Librarian of the Bodleian and presented to the conference by Dr. Goodwin were strongly in favour of readmission under severe restrictions' (*Wolf*) was swept away by the indignation of Prynne and his supporters on the very point of a hypocritical concealment of faith on the part of the 'Converso'.

Peters had, meanwhile, heard something of the Maranos in London and their Papistical dissimulation of their religion and he vigorously denounced the Jews as a 'self-seeking generation, who made but little conscience of their own principles'. Concealment of principles was not likely to commend itself to even a tolerant or moderate Puritan assembly and Cromwell's conference failed.

Menasseh ben Israel returned patiently to Amsterdam, having pleased nobody, for the Jews of the illegal settlement in London refused to pay his return journey, and Cromwell was obliged to pay it himself. What Cromwell did manage to achieve was the establishment of a synagogue in London where the Jews might worship openly and legally, and the gift of a plot of ground for legal burial.

When the Jews returned it was not upon a principle of toleration they were admitted to the country, but as a matter of convenience and expediency for another King, this time Charles II, who had been indebted to them for help during his exile and his return, and who now rewarded his chief friends among them with places of honour in his Kingdom. And so, by peaceful penetration, the Jews returned to England.

AARON.
BENCH END
LINCOLN COLL.

XII

Edmund Rich — Master of Arts and Saint
(d. 1240)

This Edmond was i-bore at Abyngdown besides Oxenforde, and had holy fadir and moder . . .
He ferde as the olyve tree that holdeth to itself the bitternesse in the rynde, and holdeth out to
other the swetnes of the oyle. Polychronicon.

WHEN I first began to inquire about Edmund Rich, the first Master of
Arts and the first Oxford Don to become a canonized Saint, my pounce
was unhappy; for I read that in dying, he washed the crucifix, drank the
water and said, 'Ye shall drink water from the wells of salvation'.

These medieval saints seem so far removed from us that they may as well have
inhabited another planet, I thought impatiently, and was prepared to relegate St.
Edmund to a stained glass window and a hagiography when I read; 'He fared as the
olive tree that holdeth to itself the bitterness in the rind and holdeth out to others the
sweetness of the oil', and I knew that anyone of whom that could be written in simplicity must have left a legacy in the hearts of men.

To a devout mind of the middle ages, the chief enemies of the soul were the bodily
desires, and the whole armour of God the austerities which subdued them; and Edmund
Rich was initiated into this belief and practice by surely the most astonishing mother
who ever bore six children.

She, too, was regarded as a saint by the people of Abingdon (where she was buried).
'A woman, she was esteemed so devoute and sainte-like, that divers zealous persons

38

St. Michael's and the Corn

thought themselves very happy if they could obtain something that belonged to her, to perpetuate not only her memory with them, but to free them from ill-fortune, charms and the like. Her gilt gyrdle with a blue corse, commonly called the long pendant gyrdle, was religiously kept by certain persons in Oxford for many years.'

It can be seen that Mabel Rich, the mother of Edmund, had her own local celebrity; and with this strange mother the conviction that Edmund, the youngest of her children, was destined to be a saint brought about a singular education for the little boy. Mabel's own austerities for herself and her family were so formidable that her less devout (or more sensible) husband gained her permission to enter a monastery as an easier place to live in than her house. She wore a hair-shirt with an iron corset on top and provided a hair-shirt for each of her children. She fasted tenaciously, as if for high prizes, and bribed tiny Edmund by toys (I wonder what they were) to eat bread and water. Eating was a waste of time — washing as much so!

A thoroughly fanatical and injudicious woman? Not in accordance with the monkish teaching of her time; only a woman setting out enthusiastically to live the religious life as she was instructed, and if that was the way to reach heaven's gate, she would see that her children trod that path with her.

Edmund, the gentle receptive child whose birth (possibly 1175) had cost her a good deal, inherited and was trained by her to this enthusiasm, but he had still his father living, and Dr. Hook (who wrote the lives of the Primates of England) believes that it was from *his* monastery that the various decisions for the child's education were issued. This is the side of Edmund Rich's life which concerns Oxford, for he was sent to one of the grammar schools of the University at the age of 12 and there is every reason to suppose that it was a school or hostel supported by his father's monastery.

The loneliness of a little boy of 12, so strictly dragooned by his mother and lacking her moral support in the strange school among other boys and men, appears in a fanciful piety very soon. The child's first purchase in Oxford was two silver rings engraved with '*Ave Maria*'. He was not going to forget, poor little soul! He found a church with an image of the Virgin which had attracted him and, placing one ring on her finger and the other on his own, he wedded the Virgin and vowed himself to celibacy. He could hardly have known what such a thing was at that age, but he had chosen his liege lady and was comforted.

Left quite alone now (for, though his mother was fanatical, one imagines there might be kind servants in the background of the home) his fasting, his hair-shirt and excess of zeal in study, for he was in this enthusiastic and immoderate also, brought brain-fever upon the child, 'He lerned his gramere and was so diseased of the headache that he had none hope to spede afterwardes in lore'.

They ordered his head to be shaved for the fever, but, his mother coming to see him, insisted upon the shaving taking the form of a tonsure and on the child's recovery she regarded it as a sign that the devout life was to be his. It never was, in the way in which she desired it, for Edmund Rich was to become a scholar who welcomed many

39

kinds of new learning disapproved of by his mother, and his ecclesiastical life was not spent in a monastery, but in high official places amid controversies and political struggles. One does not wonder that the boy walked by himself and saw heavenly visions in the Oxford meadows.

'In a tyme he walked by himself in a mede bysides Oxenforde and a faire child appeared to him and saide, "Heyle, my leef". I wonder that thou knowest me nough, and nameliche while I am alway by thy syde in schole and in other places, and therefore what thou sixt in my fore-heede, i-write; prynte it eveviche nyght in thyn owne forehead and the wytinage was "Jesus Nazarenus rex Judeorum!" Thereafter he lerned to have our Lordes passion alwey in his mynde.'

It depends so much on the attitude of mind towards these things! If one reads the early religious chronicles on St. Edmund, one sees the emphasis (admiration rather), placed on these visions of a delicate dreaming child, who, as a saint, would remain a little helpless in the midst of the world and had need of more practical people around him.

But in actual fact, few people have been less helpless than Edmund Rich who, though enthusiastic always and often unpractical did raise the standard of learning in the University at an extraordinarily difficult time and in his later status as Archbishop of Canterbury withstood both King and Pope with effectual vigour. It was no feeble if exquisite saint who uttered these words to his King. 'Examine your conscience, Sir King, for not only they who caused these letters to be sent, but all who were aware of the treachery designed, are as guilty of the Earl Marshall's murder as if with their own hands they had done the deed.' It was no dreamer of dreams who, in his office as Archbishop of Canterbury, refused the Pope's invitation to a banquet which had been too casually offered. For the garment of holiness clothes first the iron rectitude of spirit which wins the name of saint for all the great confessors, whether Edmund Rich or Elizabeth Fry. The manifestations vary.

George Herbert would feel and write,

> 'Let thy minde's sweetnesse have his operation
> Upon thy body, clothes and habitation'

and St. Edmund seldom washed. (One of the miracles recorded of him is that his hair-shirt did not harbour lice.) We now prefer the clean saint to the dirty one, but St. Edmund's contemporaries had no such predilections. It is touching, too, to find this child, so unwisely closed in by the fanaticism of his mother, in later life placing 'beauty, agility and health' among the bodily joys of heaven.

The education of Mabel Rich's sons was given to them in Paris (here again, probably at the urgency of the father) but though the Riches had abundant means, Mabel sent her sons to the French University begging their way like the friars she hoped against hope they might become. But when ideas are once scattered they become more potent than armies, and Edmund returned from France ready to teach in Oxford, not only the old church learning but the new secular and pagan authors and the excitements of mathematics.

When he returned to Oxford, the students and tutors were straggling back after the migration to Cambridge and Reading which followed the murder of four clerks by the townsmen in the reign of King John. There seems hardly to have been a University as such; rather a succession of teachers and lecturers, hiring their own lecture-rooms; sometimes teaching in the Churches or their porches; the boys living in great independence in their hostels and paying their fees to such masters as they followed. It was all very loosely held together, becoming, however, each year more of a corporate body with a central administration.

It was to this rather haphazard collection that Edmund Rich returned as a Don, quickly becoming one of the teachers most sought after and one of those about whom good stories are told.

That he took no fees except those which his 'scolers' chose to give him; that when he was offered payments he laid the money on the window-sill, saying, 'Pouder to pouder, and askes to askes'; but alas! 'the money was ofte i-take awey with his felowes in game, other els privileche with theofs'.

'He made large spences, for he would nowght be held covetous and a wretche.'

'He spend alwey more than he hadde' (again it depends on the point of view).

'For grete kneeling his knees were hard as the soles of his feet.'

He turned away the rain from a congregation who had come to hear him preach.

So the stories mount and grow, some foolish, some charming, of this unusual Oxford Don.

His time as a teacher was a happy one. Perhaps the gentle Edmund learnt as a Don the practice of authority which was to be his help against Kings and subversive ecclesiastics in his later life.

'He was a nobill prechour, a sharp arguer and a mylde lyster. For he was avised and took heed of fallas and was war and wyse in assayllnge of questionnes.'

The exciting years of his career came later as Prebendary of Salisbury and afterwards Archbishop of Canterbury. His reforms were many even in the social life of the times and he joined in the preaching of the Crusades, but his own personal Crusade lay in the upholding of the See of Canterbury against the wayward and interested appointments by King and Pope of foreign ecclesiastics. It may be that the reluctance of Pope Innocent to canonize Edmund as saint, was in part reminiscent. Yet in fact he yielded to popular feeling and it was done. But it was with his happier and earlier years that Oxford was concerned. His awe-inspiring austerities; his genuine and liberal learning; his labours to raise the level of study in the University and his great goodness — these must have been very apparent and active to have left such an impression on the minds of his students in a few short years of teaching.

41

XIII

'When Michael Scot was Young'

Rose-sheathed beside the rosebud tongue
Lurks the young adder's tooth;
Milk-mild from new-born hemlock-bluth
The earliest drops are wrung
And sweet the flower of his first youth
When Michael Scot was young.

D. G. ROSSETTI

Quell' altro, che ne' fianchi è così poco
Michele Scotto fu, che veramente
delle magiche frode seppe il gioco.

DANTE

AFTER the singing of angelic hosts appear the frosty wastes of hell! Edmund the saint has his dark counterpart in the Oxford undergraduate who walks in the eighth circle of Dante's Inferno. Michael Scot, tight-waist and all, was allotted a place there among the wizards, necromancers and sorcerers who, in punishment for their unhallowed curiosity about the future, are ordained to walk for ever with their heads twisted on their necks, looking eternally backwards.

I confess that the evidence (apart from the tradition) of Michael Scot's ever having been at Oxford goes largely by default. Such shadowy reasons as may be brought to that interesting plea are as follows.

'Roger Bacon shows great familiarity with Scot, and Bacon was an Oxford scholar though his studies at that University were not begun till after the time when Scot could possibly have been a student there. It is quite possible, however, that the interest shown by Bacon in Scot's labours and high reputation — not by any means of a kindly sort — may have been awakened by traditions that were still current in the schools of Oxford when the younger student came there. Near the end of his life Scot visited, in a public capacity, the chief Universities of Europe, and brought them philosophic treasures that were highly thought of by the learned. It seems most probable from the terms in which Bacon speaks of this journey that it may have included a visit to Oxford "(Tempore Michaelis Scoti, qui, annis 1230 transactis, apparuit, deferens librorum Aristotelis partes aliquas)". This might, of course, be matter of mere duty and policy, but one cannot help observing how well it agrees with the tradition that these schools were already familiar to Scot. As a recognized alumnus of Oxford he would be highly acceptable there, being one whose European fame shed no small lustre upon the scene of his early studies.' (*Life and legend of M. Scot: Rev. J. Wood Brown.*)

42

Carfax from the Mitre

So that if Michael Scot wasn't educated at Oxford he evidently ought to have been. Let's consider him!

When one reads of wizards in the dawn of learning, a strange book is one sure sign of commerce with demons; one expects, too, mathematical inquiries, a study of the heavens and a secret addiction to Aristotle.

They were all present in Michael Scot — the words of power, the mighty book, the art that none may name, all these give a shuddering swing to the *Lay of the Last Minstrel*.

> 'Now speed thee what thou hast to do,
> Or, Warrior, we may dearly rue,
> For those thou mayst not look upon
> Are gathering fast by the yawning stone!
> Then Deloraine in terror took
> From the cold hand the Mighty Book;
> With iron clasped and with iron bound,
> He thought as he took it, the dead man frowned.'

Yet when the goblin-page stole the book from the knight and managed to prize open the clasp and read a few lines, they scarcely seem to have warranted all that crowding of demons around the tomb.

> 'And one short spell therein he read.
> It had much of glamour might
> Could make a ladye seem a knight,
> The cobwebs on a dungeon wall
> Seem tapestry in a lordly hall;
> A nutshell seem a gilded barge,
> A shieling seem a palace large,
> And youth seem age and age seem youth,
> All was delusion, naught was truth.'

Rossetti inclined to the 'Merlin and Lady' legend of Michael Scot. Tales of his familiar demon are common in Scotland, his native land, but the shrewd may observe that the demon is almost always being dispatched by Scot to go and play somewhere else, and it transpires that very few men of his time actually occupied so many respectable and reputable positions. At Paris he became Master and was known as Michael the Mathematician. He took orders. Later he was offered a bishopric. He was appointed tutor (probably in mathematics) to the delicate boy who afterwards became the Emperor Frederick II of Palermo in Sicily, and was to transmit to him the same enthusiasm for scientific inquiry which he himself possessed. He wrote books on hygiene and medicine and a volume de luxe on health and morals for the guidance of his pupil before his marriage. He withdrew to Toledo to join the school of translators established in that city by the learned Archbishop of Toledo, Primate of Spain. He translated the whole works of the Arabian follower of Aristotle, Averroes, and then returned to Palermo as Court-Astrologer to his old pupil, now the Emperor, a highly respectable appointment in those days. By the Emperor's advice his translation of Averroes remained unpublished, the spread of books and of curious knowledge having attracted the animosity of the narrower type of Churchman.

In the corner of a fresco in the Church of Santa Maria Novella in Florence is a small figure with peaked cap, girt waist and pointed beard. All eyes are fixed upon the Friar who is exhorting to repentance — all save Michael Scot the wizard, who in the corner is hard at work repenting, tearing up the condemned book of philosophy of which he is the translator. That is how Michael Scot appeared to the Church in the dawn of learning and since Dante was a ghibelline of the same political faction as Scot's master the Emperor Frederick, it was 'not political but moral disapproval' which placed Scot in the Inferno. (Unless indeed Dante ran short of sorcerers for his Canto, and found it wiser to insert a dead-and-gone foreigner rather than a living necromancer.)

It was more than a revival, it was a great surging of delight which flooded the world of scholars at the discovery of the natural sciences by way of translation from the Arabian authors. The schools of Toledo were not the first of their kind, for the books now undergoing translation in Spain were long ago translated from the Greek by the Arabian doctors.

'Mamoun', a Prince extraordinarily intelligent and of an inquiring and liberal mind, 'founded at Bagdad about 217 A.D. an official bureau of translators in the Palace of Wisdom. At the head of this bureau was set an eminent scholar Hvêrn, son of Isaac. The son of a doctor, he was born 194 A.D. As a young man he went to Bagdad where he followed the lectures of a well-known physician but as he was too tiresome a questioner one day his master refused to answer him. He then journeyed to Byzantine territory — remaining two years to learn Greek and acquire a collection of scientific books. He returned to Bagdad travelling to Persia and Basra to perfect his Arabic and so back to his home in Bagdad to begin his translations'. (*Life of Avicennes*.) Truly, learning and books were esteemed in those days. The Tower of Babel was being demolished stone by stone.

The scholars caught fire! Translating was the only work and they fell to it earnestly. The schools of Egypt and Persia had taken from the Greek philosophers, adding their own contribution of mathematics, astronomy, medicine and natural philosophy. The world had become boundless in interest and colour. The Jews, themselves greatly advanced in medicine, with their facility in language, and their ubiquity, were often the link between the Oriental and the Latin.

'You have then,' said Avendeath (a Jewish translator), 'the book which has been translated from the Arabic according to your commands, I reading it word by word in the vernacular (Spanish) and Dominic the archdeacon rendering it word by word into Latin.'

It was a complicated process, and if it was rendered word by word into a third language by a scribe who understood only imperfectly, it might lead to corrupt texts, yet it went on ceaselessly. Renan calls attention in his life of Averroes to this loosing of books on the world.

'One of the most singular phenomena of the history of literature in the Middle Ages, is the activity of intellectual exchange and the rapidity with which books spread from one end to the other of Europe. So that a work compiled in Morocco or in Cairo, was known in Paris in less time than it would take in our day for an important German book to cross the Rhine.'

From such a clearing-house as Toledo these books poured forth, distributing new knowledge, knowledge at first of the natural sciences and mathematics. The chart and study of the heavens were hailed with the delight of children at the sight of a new picture-book. The natural world was alive and awake and for a while all went happily with the scholars. Then by degrees, all the simmering and smelting and calculating and forecasting and the strange symbols of triangles and figures seemed to be tinged with infernal flame, and a laboratory became a workshop of the black and magic arts. The burning of books began!

In 1192 a certain doctor was accused of atheism and his books condemned to be burnt. Rabbi Juda, the beloved disciple of Maimonides, was witness in Madrid of this strange scene.

'I saw,' he declared, 'in the hands of the priest, a work on astronomy by Ibn-el-Haitum. Displaying the circle by which the author represented the celestial globe, "Behold," he said, "the awful rascality, the incalculable evil, the black curse!" and saying these words he tore the book apart and threw it on the fire.' (*Life of Avicennes: Renan.*)

The scholars committed to research began to show open contempt for the Church and when, in spite of his cautious diplomacy towards the Pope, the Emperor Frederick excited his displeasure by luke-warmness towards the Crusades, he cared no further to placate a suspicious Authority, but, being an Emperor proceeded to do as he pleased, and one of the things he was pleased to do was to allow his court astrologer to publish his translation of Averroes, held over for ten years.

No Queen of Sheba is ever reported to have journeyed to the court of Frederick at Palermo where Michael Scot officially studied the heavens, and is reported to have made such investigations into the movements of matter that a form of seismograph was invented, but the court must have been as full of wonders as that of King Solomon.

The interest in the life and habits of animals led the Emperor to collect a magnificent Zoo; absorption in the movements of the planets and in the science of mathematics, brought the magi of Egypt to the court in strange garments. Michael Scot is said to have adopted the Eastern sage's robes. With all this exotic dress and behaviour, the Court of Frederick soon became the workshop of infernal powers, Beelzebub was the Emperor's messenger, Lucifer his footman. What wonder that a slightly embittered if urbane little man who possessed all the necessary qualifications for a wizard (he had even been said to have sought speech with the dead Averroes at Cordoba) should give his belated translation of the philosopher to a world already primed to attack it. Thence came indifference and contempt. The burning of books no more hinders the spreading of knowledge than the blinking of an owl disturbs the sunrise. The books of Averroes were burnt, but more books were added to 'the making of many books of which there is no end'.

Michael Scot was honoured in the Universities of Europe. In his native land of Scotland to which he returned, his image is as shadowy as the mist and his reputed activities as incalculable. He set his familiar demon the task of weaving ropes of sand on Berwick shore. Perhaps he is at it now.

MAGICIAN
RECANTING
SANTA MARIA NOTELLA
FLORENCE

XIV

Joyce Frankland — Merchant's Wife (1531-1587)

What is good for a bootless bene?
The Falconer to the Lady said.
And she made answer 'Endless sorrow!'
For she knew that her Son was dead.

WORDSWORTH

JOYCE FRANKLAND was a mother of the sixteenth century, who one day received suddenly and terribly the broken body of her only son; a familiar figure enough now after years of war, the mother mourning her son, dead by violence, but unlooked for and calamitous in the life of peace and in the home of a wealthy woman who was preparing to give her only son all possible outgoings.

At the age of twenty-three, William Saxey, her son by her first husband, a merchant-venturer, was thrown from a young horse which he was trying to break in, and instantly killed. The shock and bereavement bore down the simple kindly woman and so the kind Dean of St. Paul's, Dean Nowell, found her, half-demented and wholly possessed by sorrow.

'I think it was of God', he writes simply, that the suggestion came to him. The suggestion, in fact, stayed the poor mother's weeping and thence restored her reason.

'Comfort yourself, good Mrs. Frankland, and I will tell you how you shall have twenty good sons to comfort you in these your sorrowes which you take for your owne sonne.'

The poor lady stopped her crying to listen, and the result was her ultimate determination, 'in lieu of her most loving sonne William, to raise and to beget unto herself, in vertue and lerning many children'.

She was a goldsmith's daughter, the widow of a merchant-venturer, the present wife of a rich merchant in cloth — not a trace of the great lady about her, only a kind mother of the middle class, bitterly bereaved, and setting about with a quiet will to do for other women's sons what she would never again do for her own. That is how Joyce Frankland appears in Oxford history.

Had she lived three centuries earlier, she would probably have been persuaded to build a chantrey or a church or to endow a nunnery, but in her day there were few nunneries and fewer chantries or prayers for the dead, and it was not an unknown thing in her own family to endow colleges and found scholarships for poor boys, for her mother Johanna Trapps, wife of the famous London goldsmith, Ralph Trapps, and an heiress in her own right, had already founded certain fellowships in the University.

I do not know to what rallying-point a family motto may bring its members, but the motto of the Trapps family to which Mrs. Joyce Frankland belonged was the noble legend 'Suffer and Serve', and in effect, from the moment Joyce Frankland stilled her weeping to listen to Dean Nowell, this motto became alive and active for her.

'They would be in love to you as deare children and heartily pray to God for you during your life', said the kind Dean and it is now some four hundred years since Mrs. Frankland's son was carried home dead, and still in the Grace after meat on the Gaudy night at Brasenose College (where most of her benefactions were bestowed) the name of Jocosa Frankland is remembered by the 'sonnes in vertue and lerning' to whom she opened her heart when her son's death left it empty.

To the mother of Edmund Rich, three centuries earlier, there could have been no greater contrast than Joyce Frankland. Her portrait shows her well-coloured, well-nourished, well-dressed. A hair-shirt would fill her with disgust. She wears jewels, fine ones, as a goldsmith's daughter would, and holds in her hand the fashionable watch called a 'Nuremberg egg'.

She displays the watch to her 'sonnes' — 'The time is short', she would tell them. She herself bequeathed her portrait to the Colleges (in Cambridge also) to which she bequeathed her magnificent gifts. Her many sons in learning should feel her a presentable mother.

Poor mother! I thought as I read her will, that in the very thoroughness with which she fulfilled her resolution she found some comfort. A woman whose portrait displays such competent comeliness and dignity would be an excellent *chatelaine* of her town and country houses. (She was for a while the owner of the famous Rye House), and to have arranged with such detail for the comforts and commons of so many of her 'deare sons' must have warmed her heart and brought satisfaction into her stricken life.

Her fortune was very great. Her mother, as was said, had been an heiress, and the fact that Thomas Cromwell the Lord Chancellor had dealings with her father the famous goldsmith, of itself suggests large monies. Nothing niggardly lurked in the family tradition and Joyce Frankland's money was handsomely used.

Her chief benefactions in Oxford were given to Brasenose College (1586). But Lincoln also shared her generosity. The wonderful gift of plate which she bequeathed to Brasenose was stolen, but her lands accumulated in value.

Now and then, in Oxford conversations, I have heard a disparaging of wealthy tradesmen who endow (or wish to) some side of a learned profession, as if no one less august than a medieval archbishop ever left his money to a College. Oxford owes much to great ecclesiastics, to princes and queens and great ladies but there is a good deal to be said of the men who made fortunes in trade — Tesdale the maltster of Abingdon; Thomas White, the Merchant Taylor; Ralph Trapps, the London goldsmith. Mr. Thomas Knolle, a London grocer, gave books to Bodley's Library. A nation of shop-keepers should not omit to give thanks for the generosity of merchants as well as princes.

Grace at Brasenose

Joyce Frankland had no great ambition, only a desire to set other boys on the way and to give them the same comforts she would have given her son. I wonder if she ever thought that unlike most mothers' sons, these sons of her perpetual adoption never grew older than her dead boy. Generations succeeded one another, but she could always be certain that William Saxey, aged 23, would be represented in every one.

Grace after meat (*recited on the night of the gaudy dinner at Brasenose*).

'*Qui nos creavit redemit et pavit sit benedictus in aeternum. Deus exaudi orationem nostram. Agimus tibi gratias, Pater caelestis, pro Gulielmo Smyth, episcopo, et Ricardo Sutton, milite, fundatoribus nostris, pro Alexandro Nowell et Jocosa Frankland alisque benefactoribus nostris, humiliter Te precantes ut numerum eorum benignissime adaugeas. Ecclesiam Catholicam et populum Christianum custodi. Haereses et errores omnes extirpa. Elizabetham Reginam nostram et subditos eius defende. Pacem da et conserva per Christum Dominum nostrum.*'

XV

The Kindly Fruits of the Earth

ALL summer I have laboured obediently over the kindly fruits of the earth that in these times of hard going for sailor men, I may make myself and my household independent of public supplies. I know to a nicety how many earwigs a cabbage can support, and where the thrush gets through to my ripening currants, I know that if I pick the plums from half of the tree and leave the rest for another time there will *be* no other time, for the blackbird will see to that. I watch sadly those 'kitchen lilies' the onions, wilting with some interior rot. I make jelly of the Japanese quince and of parsley. I am acquainted with man's primal curse. 'In the sweat of my face' I (very occasionally) 'eat my bread.'

Nothing could have been further from my imagining than that war should bring about my very gates a waving and delicate beauty, yet instead of a desolate waste of land full of weeds and vermin, there now stretches to my door the incredible soft gold of a summer cornfield, an illumination even on a starry night. All through this amazing summer of heat it has entertained the sun, sturdy and ruddy-ripe.

There is a thudding now the autumn has fallen as if some war-plane climbed above us. But it is a sound of ancient days long before the war, of the thresher and his machine; and it is the full sheaves which climb the ladder pouring their white grain on the ground. This ritual of harvest is a long and learned one. The whisking of dry straw and the cascading of grain goes on all day until the men appear as pigmies by the side of their work. The stack grows visibly, blocking the sky. The bountiful heap becomes like water to wade in, the chaff thigh deep. A glistening dust like a galaxy of motes entangles the sunshine. A halo covers earth's plenty. So antique are the ritual and the gestures, the grain tossed by shovels, the men building the sheaves, the pigmies raising a mountain — that harvest seems even in the midst of war the only concern of mankind. The casketted grain is piled upon the wagon. The clumsy, clever engines are quiet. Night cannot make quieter the things they leave behind.

XVI

Pie - Powders

Is this well, goody Joan, to interrupt my market in the midst and take away my customers? Can you answer this at the pie-poudres?

BEN JONSON

To regulate the currency, to secure the country against the loss of specie, and more harmlessly, to prevent the importation of spurious or debased coin, the officers of the King's exchange examined into the mercantile transactions of the foreign traders. To form a ready remedy against fraud, the mayor sat at his 'court of the dusty feet'. There was no appeal from his judgement.

THOROLD ROGERS, History of Agriculture and Prices

'LA Salle des pas perdus' of Méryon's etching is a hall of gloom, but the court of the dusty feet (pieds poudrés) of the Medieval Fair must have been a noisy and vivid assembly. I confess that when I first heard of Pie-Powders in connection with ancient Fairs, I thought they were something to eat, like Deddington Pudding-pies which one bought only on the occasion of that Fair; and the fact that pie-powders were men, men with 'dusty feet' and therefore travelling pedlars and merchants, with a special court of justice in the Fair called the Pie-Powders' Court which checked and redressed their wrongs (or the wrongs they had done to others) within the hour, aroused my curiosity about these Fairs and their overseas traders which I took pains to satisfy.

I remember an entertaining hour spent with the late Mr. Gunther in his scientific instruments room in the Old Ashmolean. Unlocking one case, he brought out what appeared to be only a silver-gilt crucifix of beautiful work, mounted on a base of three steps; such a private object of devotion as had been carried from town to town by a well-to-do merchant. To our astonishment the crucifix carried other uses than that of devotion. A tiny spring, when pressed, extended the arms to the length of a foot measure. A pin loosed at the top showed the shaft to be hollow, containing delicate instruments for measuring and cutting. The steps were drawers with apothecary weights and a scale for the weighing of gold pieces, and on the back a tiny gnomon, attached by a minute chain, with the numerals cut on the shaft and the steps, told our man of the dusty feet the time of day in the centuries before the usage of clocks. There were others in the museum, crosses and crucifixes and a small portable altar, carved with great precision and skill and all serving several functions beside that of devotion. The merchant with the dusty feet was often, in the Middle Ages, a man of substance and ingenuity. The Fairs to which these travelling merchants came were not markets as we know them today. The market was of regular occurrence. The Fair only occurred on occasions, sometimes only once a year. The date of the Fair often coincided with

52

a Saint's day and Feast, when the people would be flocking to the Festival in any case. The market traded in merchandise of the country; the Fair was the only place where foreign merchandise could be bought.

'It will be remembered that the regular process of distribution by retail shops with which we are so familiar, had in those days no existence except perhaps in the greater towns. It was only on special occasions, that is to say at Fairs and Markets, that any want could be supplied. It was by these means only that surplus produce could be disposed of.' (*T. Rogers.*)

It is curious to reflect upon the complicated history we inherit, even in our most ordinary customs. It was even so long ago as the days of Canute that a law was passed forbidding the sale of any article of higher value than 4d. without the presence of witnesses. 'Some unlying man' must bear witness that there has been no attempt to evade the revenue tax by selling in secret what has a tax imposed upon it. Hence the rise of markets to ensure buying and selling in appointed places under the King's licence and with the inspection of the officers of weights and measures. But the great Fairs were the occasion of the entry of the foreign trader. Large sums of money passed. Defoe mentions that the sum of £100,000 changed hands at one stall in one week at the Stourbridge Fair at Cambridge. He speaks of the Fair ground half a mile square divided into streets, of warehouses or booths three stories high and of an incredible medley of folk. The Fairs were so profitable to the owners of the ground, that there was much rivalry to obtain the Royal Licence for a Fair. Very often the great Abbeys and religious Foundations, with their approaches and bridges kept in good repair and often placed near a convenient water-way, gained an excellent revenue from the yearly Fair held on their estates. Some Fairs were private ventures, and the Crown enriched its Treasury by the holding of Fairs. Sometimes they supported a Charity and the lease of the ground for the famous Stourbridge Fair was King John's endowment of a hospital for lepers. But they were invariably held for the display and purchase of foreign merchandise which could be bought in no other way.

The Leipzig Fair is, I suppose, the chief survival of the kind of Fair which used to bring men of the dusty feet to all parts of England, and which brought such heavy profit to the proprietors of any Fair ground.

The men of the dusty feet 'came from the Baltic with furs and amber. They arrived from Genoa with silks and velvets. France sent enamel and goldsmith's work. Venice sent glass — Norway tar; and Spain traded iron; Turkey sent figs and spice. Cinnamon and pepper, saffron and ginger were carried in ships from the East and traded in England'. One can see how the Pie-Powders changed the face of England in their periodic incursions, and they in their turn took back the solid English goods, especially woollen stuffs, brass ware and iron goods.

The shops of adjacent towns were closed when the Pie-Powders brought goods to the Fair. Nobles and wealthy men came from great distances to buy 'things of complaisance' which they could buy nowhere else. Bailiffs of Colleges bought a whole

53

year's plenishing and the merchants themselves left the Fair ground and the country with money enough to have made their journey worth while or to carry their dusty feet to the next available Fair. There were shows at the Fair and toys and trinkets, and the whole often ended with a horse-show.

As might be expected, foreign trading was jealously regarded by the merchant at home, and appeals for protection from the swamping of English trade by foreign goods were as loud in the days of King John as they are today.

Restrictions were set upon the length of time a foreign trader might linger in the country and proceedings on this point were frequent.

'Alien merchants should come only to the "four fairs" and should not remain in England more than forty days.'

The powerful German Hanseatic League bullied its way to special preference and its merchants seemed to stay as long as they pleased, but not without loud protest, and on the small foreign trader a strict eye was kept. The Court of Pie-Powder redressed the wrongs of the local people from the exactions of the men of the dusty feet and the peace of the Fairs was kept. England was, in fact, the first country to grant easy terms to the foreign merchant and the seven points of Henry in 1216 were a virtual adumbration of free trade and in spite of a somewhat see-saw legislation, the Pie-Powders themselves have always been a source of revenue to English traders.

It is safe then to think of our 'dusty foot' of the handsome crucifix, setting off to the Fairs of England from Venice or Genoa — perhaps he took the Fairs of France on the way, it may be he came through the Low Countries. With his scissors and measures tucked away in his crucifix, he may have sold silk or velvet. He would disembark his bales perhaps at Blakeney, always travelling by water wherever possible. 'The merchants who frequent the water between London and Oxford used to have free passage on the Thames from London to Oxford with their ships to carry their goods and to serve the commonalty and the people, but now they are disturbed by weirs, locks, mills and many other hindrances...' There was better protection from robbers on the water-ways also, and freight was cheaper.

So our dusty foot would disembark his goods as near the Fair ground as he could. He would find the 'street' of the Fair assigned to those who sold his kind of merchandise. He, dealing in silks, would wait until the cloth-merchants had finished. In turn he would give place to the dealers in wool and in wool-fels. The roads would be like the roads to Epsom on Derby Day. The tolls for roads and bridges and for right to sell at the Fair would be diligently gathered in. For his own merchandise there would be its own special tax. He would meet merchants from other foreign countries and exchange views and politics. He would buy English goods to fill his ships returning from Lynn to the Low Countries, goods to sell again at home. He might stay to buy a horse for further English journeys at the horse fair at the end, and have to use his wits to know whether he was buying a stolen horse or not. International goodwill might be carried by the Pie-Powders in a special manner. A nation of shop-keepers can purvey Peace

St. Giles Fair

among its wares. Later perhaps, most important of all, our merchant brought books to St. Giles' Fair in Oxford, for in the sixteenth century after the spread of printing, books were an important article of sale. A fascinating study would be the spread of news of books and pamphlets at these Fairs in the days before the newspaper was invented. D. Thorold Rogers has an illuminating passage on this very point of the sale of books at St. Giles' Fair.

'In the latter part of the period before me, the Fair of the North Hundred of Oxford, held at the beginning of September, though it never approached the dimensions of Stourbridge, was a famous place for the sale of books. New works were virtually published at Fairs, and it is in this way, I think, that we can account for the publication and distribution of that mass of literature which, issued after the period comprised within these volumes, is so remarkably copious. By what means, for instance, could the exceedingly numerous works of Prynne have been distributed? In what manner did the publisher or printer reach his customers? Advertisements were unknown. Patrons and subscription-lists were equally matters of the future. But books were got at and probably through these Fairs, which were exceedingly numerous in the Autumn months, and where, even though the book were unlicensed and considered dangerous, the dealer and purchaser found means to know one another. I have more than once found entries of purchases for College Libraries with a statement that the book was bought at St. Giles' Fair. Unfortunately, as that which is familiar to one generation is being lost to another, no note is taken of the change, as no note is made of the circumstance when the fact is customary. But few inquiries would be more curious or instructive than the history of English Fairs when the practice was universal and the facts were significant. They begin at a very remote time, and were probably instituted on those border districts, which, being no-man's land, lay outside the mark, and therefore were neutral territory, in which a special jurisdiction, the Court of the Pie-Powder, had to be established. Like valuable privileges, they soon became a franchise and were a considerable source of revenue to those who could appropriate the right of permitting a temporary occupancy. After having served the most important ends, they have at last become nothing but a scene of coarse and rude amusement and almost a nuisance. But the change is little more than a generation old.' St. Giles' Fair, nevertheless, though bearing the medieval name, was not a Fair but a 'Wake'. 'It took place in the Manor of Walton outside the city walls, and still occupies its traditional site in St. Giles and Magdalen Street. This manor belonged in the Middle Ages to Godstow Nunnery and passed to St. John's College after the dissolution of the monasteries' (*Hole*). In 1773 Sir John Peshall wrote, 'At present we have no Fair. A wake is at St. Giles' called St. Giles' Wake yearly, the Monday after St. Giles' Day', but Miss Hole comments, 'Many of the Charters granted by the Norman Kings to the monasteries and other Lords of the Manor confirmed an already well-established fair rather than created a new one. Where no such Charter was given the market frequently continued without it and gained the name of "Fair" by custom. St. Giles' in Oxford is an example of this. It never had a charter yet it has outlived the regular chartered Fairs of the City'.

There had been five chartered fairs in Oxford. 'St. Frideswide's Fair' whose charter was granted by Henry I to the Priory of that name; the 'May Fair' granted by Edward IV to the Austin Friars, and three whose charters were granted by Queen Elizabeth to the city. Of these past Fairs the most important was that of St. Frideswide and its authority was vested in the Canons of Christ Church. The legal document is wordy and long but it makes clear provision for the 'Court of Pepowders'. The rights of the Fair were sold to the Burgesses of Oxford.

'St. Frideswide's Fair in a short time was surrendered to the King with other pro-perties of King Henry VIII's College and was sold by the Crown to the Burgesses of Oxford for more than £300. The deed of purchase is entered in the Vellum Book in the city Archives.' (*Salter.*)

Traces of the Pie-Powders Court, though now chiefly of an ornamental and cere-monial significance can be found, I am told, at the 'Dirty' or 'October' Fair at Market Drayton; at Newcastle, Ely, Newbury and Guildford. At Bristol the ceremony which takes place was initiated in 1413. Its significance is now slight but every year the ser-geant at Mace of the City of Bristol calls the Proclamation. 'All manner of persons having anything to do at this Court of the Pie-Poudre for the City and County of Bristol held and kept there this day in the old market, draw near and give your atten-dance!' Since no one ever has any business now, dismissal is proclaimed. 'All manner of persons who have anything further to do at this Court of the Pie-Poudres for the City and County of Bristol held and kept here this day and in the old market may now depart hence and give their attendance at the Tolzey Court Office forthwith. God save the King!'

The Mulberry, Merton Fellows' Garden

XVII

'Here we go round the Mulberry Bush'

And they showed the elephants the blood of grapes and of mulberries that they might prepare them for battle.   1 *Maccabees vi.* 34

IF it had not been for the late war and its severe scrutiny of waste, there would never have been so many friends gathering round the College mulberry trees. They grow in the old Dolphin garden, once the garden of an Inn, now a quiet place absorbed into the sanctuary of a College enclosure.

It may be that the planting of a mulberry tree in so many old Inn gardens is due as John Evelyn says to the 'extraordinary care' of King James I, who did 'recommend it to this nation, by a book of directions, acts of council and all other princely assistance. But this did not take, no more than that of Henry IV's proposal about the environs of Paris, who filled the highways, parks and gardens of France with the trees, beginning in his own garden for encouragement'. But the silk industry, which, by the planting of mulberries and the breeding of silk-worms, both monarchs tried to capture for their own country, only succeeded in France, 'to our shame be it spoken', continues John Evelyn, with some severe words upon our 'sloth and lack of industry'. Yet the trees remained, and here they were now part of the College property and production, dropping their soft black smoky fruit in the utmost prodigality all over the lawn. The deputy-keeper of the College Groves looked at the fruit, appreciated the waste and called for help. He 'wrote to the papers'. What a delightful flocking and fluttering of letters came about the mulberry trees! One could write whole family histories just on their evidence.

Someone remembered with longing a mulberry tree in the country garden she still called home. A 'College Servant' remembered the mulberry and apple dumplings of his own College. The College Chef remembered giving a rather difficult Don a mulberry pie on one occasion, 'and he never forgave me'. 'It was introduced into this country by the Romans', wrote a learned countryman. 'We used it as syrup for sore throats', said a very old lady. 'Of the fig tribe, not of the blackberry', pronounced the botanist. Kind friends came up from the village with cookery books, for the worst of having the ultra-modern is that such authorities take no heed of the antique mulberry planted by the Romans. Delicate Victorian handwriting copied recipes from their mother's journals. I do not believe that the wine-berries or cloud-berries of modern cultivation would have produced a prettier flock of letters. The telephone rang. Pleasant voices spoke. There was 'the sound of a going in the tops of the mulberry trees'. In the end there were bottled mulberries; mulberry jam, and, delectable enough to enchant even a College dessert, mulberry ices.

If anyone has any further doubts as to the friendliness and pleasant feeling in the world, let him go and look at the mulberry trees in the old Dolphin garden and be admonished.

XVIII

Period Piece

I wonder how many hundreds of empty niches there are in Oxford! Does anyone suppose that in nine cases out of ten, the architect ever expected them to be filled? Are we such a statue loving people? Do we produce so many sculptors? Is the Oxford climate so delightfully adapted to the preservation of the human face in stone?

E. W. B. NICHOLSON

How is it, I asked, that it would give us no pleasure to own any piece of furniture coming from our own father's houses, and yet among our most valued pieces are those from the generation before them — our grand-parents' furniture. At what precise time, and why, was there such a complete change in taste and even material? The excellence of workmanship in Victoria's days was beyond reproach. Those huge mahogany wardrobe doors moved on silk. The doors of the side-boards with their deeply undercut carving were as noiseless. No drawer ever got stuck or wedged. The pier-glasses had no flaw and their elaborate gilt frames no blemish. The Venetian blinds, the chandeliers, the cornices, the horse-hair sofas and bolster pillows, what of them? 'Good of their kind', we say, and collect the best of them as 'Period Pieces', implying in the phrase, I think, that the Period is completely rounded off and done with.

It is not easy to determine what makes for change of taste and ornament in any one period. How, for instance, did the Meadow buildings of Christ Church come to be built, with a Hanseatic house propped up on top as a gable, and its deplorable balconies boasted for carving which was never carved? Why should we now shy away from the Museum and prefer the Library of Queen's College? The work on the Museum was as carefully done, under the direction of Ruskin, as the carving of Grinling Gibbons. Special carvers of the old craftsman type were brought from Ireland. The O'Shea brothers were ingenious and unspoilt enough for anyone. Veritable wild-flowers were procured and copied to the life (displaying sincerity). One hundred and twenty-five varied marbles were chosen in appropriate geological sequence for the columns. The serious native gothic which housed all high spiritual thought was preferred — and yet!

One cannot, it seems, pull a period sharply back to something whose impetus is either dead or dying. But incongruities alone do not make for bad taste. Inigo Jones built a classic front on the gothic church of old St. Paul's and no one shuddered. The baroque porch on the perpendicular church of St. Mary the Virgin scarcely offends. There are interesting variations of taste within Oxford even in one lifetime, for Dr.

59

Radcliffe pays for the classic Rotunda of the Camera by Gibbs at one time and for a new gothic front to University College at another.

Perhaps one mark of a piece of bad architecture is that it is covered with 'Features', as if the architect kept a note-book of interesting details he has seen on holiday, and works them one by one into his own buildings, like a schoolgirl who fills her head with impressive quotations immediately before the examination and works them by hook or by crook into her papers — presumably to draw the attention of the examiners from any insufficient structure of learning beneath them. This gumming-on of features is a real architectural misdemeanour and one sees it displayed painfully in the meadow front of Christ Church. The material is as good as any other in Oxford and if 'the only excuse for folly is to be resolute therein' the perpetrators are resolute enough. It is the veritable *bulwark* of a Period which stands facing the Meadows.

Is it the idea of plate-glass in gothic windows which sets one's teeth on edge; Victorian domestic comfort medievally housed? It cannot all be blamed on the age of Victoria, though that period *did* sprinkle the Highlands with turretted feudal seats and castles. For there is a pleasant stretch of domestic building of that time which includes plain stucco country-houses with pillared porches and long windows and much of London's less fashionable stucco of that reign is quite agreeable to look at.

A pretentiousness which attempts to have the best of all ways has its part in this question of bad taste. By a chance the real Gothic is within a stone's throw of the pseudo Gothic and both visible from the Broad Walk. A comparison may be illuminating.

The Library of Merton is a building of early Gothic simplicity and serviceableness. There is a strong wall for containing the apartment; a steep roof with wide eaves heavily charged with stone slabs for carrying the rain and snow clear of the walls, the minimum width of window for that unglazed century; all as utilitarian as a factory, but how pleasant to look at with its tranquil spaces of walling, its solemn roof and its lights disposed with the economy necessary to the times. Suppose, without interfering with the spaciousness of the rooms of Christ Church, one filled those long staircase lights with stone walling, the appearance of stability and therefore dignity would be at once enhanced. Suppose the balconies, too small for use, were sheared from the windows, one could then discover whether three different kinds of Gothic window helped the effect; whether the attempt at Tudor chimney stacks was a mistake; why most of the stone boasted for carving should have remained unworked, and whether the house with the corbie-steps hoisted aloft would have been better on the ground.

Pretentiousness and features! These are the real lapses in taste in the Meadow building. The hewn stone is good material, and though the Gothic is our native growth, it can display an unconscionably dull façade. There are stretches of Gothic walls and windows in Oxford Colleges as dull as any in the country, but they quite evidently never pretended to be otherwise than solid walls to contain rooms with the minimum expenditure.

France contains much domestic Gothic, and Belgium its fine civic buildings. But in the cloth-hall at Ypres, the many windows were severely in one style; and where in domestic building the lights are full of tracery, they are grouped with discretion and the solid wall allowed its contribution to effect.

Time with its whirligig sees to the revolutions of taste safely enough. I have just been reading a plea for the saving of architecture in Oxford dated forty years ago and find that the Museum is the established pattern of excellence and Cockerell's building of the Ashmolean Gallery is deplored to its last stone.

Years ago, when I submitted manuscripts to professors for judgment, someone (I never knew who) pronounced this wise conclusion — 'She seems to be one who has not yet had time to acquire *a just simplicity of style*'. A just simplicity of style! Is that what is wanted for taste, in architecture or elsewhere? Why should not the detailed decoration on the Science Museum, that solemnly executed Doge's Palace, that poem in geology, convey the happy contentment of the lovely Chapter-house in Southwell Minster? Yet it doesn't!

Now and again a librarian or kindly Fellow will unearth for one plans and drawings of College buildings which were designed, considered and then rejected. Brasenose *might* have had a Crown Steeple; a façade like St. George's Hall, Liverpool; or offered a Palais de Justice to the High. It would be an amusing exercise for some clever person to reconstruct this *Oxford which was never built*. The cautionary effect might be excellent.

> 'Some raise a front up to the church
> Like old Westminster Abbey:
> And then they think the Lord to cheat
> And build the back part shabby.'
>
> (*Pugin's Contrasts*.)

XIX

'Oranges on the Trees'

Order issued by the Lords 1591.
They have noticed some neglect of the order against playing on the Sabbath day, and have observed that performances on Thursdays are a greater hurte & destruction of the game of beare-baytinge and like pastimes, which are maintayned for her Maiesties pleasure yff occasion require. On these two days therefore, they direct that no plaies be allowed, for the greater reverence of God and the encouragement of the Queen's beare-baiters.

DIMMED by twilight and moths, the trees in the windless evening carried the golden fruit as lightly as a momentary bird. The stars, elusive and glancing, were already at hand, pointed and attentive. The few human figures moving between the trees seemed in their fantasy to have slipped from lost centuries to lay Shakespeare's comedy in the College garden. Very easily the properties were set. For background there was the antiquity of great trees; for canopy the eternal heaven and the green-shadowed lawn was the stage. The speech was our noblest speech, the wit our merriest! The purple tree, immense and motionless, poised like a universe behind the players; so small, so gay and entreating, tangling and re-tracing their wits beneath the quick stars and the blue tides of heaven — and all of it — the centuries of young men and make-believe in the college garden, was gathered up in the eager question out of the twilight, 'Did you see how we did it? We hung oranges on the trees!' Thus in an English summer evening and in an Oxford College garden, Messina and warm Sicilian nights were created before our eyes.

Looking back to origins, one wonders whether the loveliest intonations of English speech would ever have been written had modern mechanical contrivance and lighting been available in Shakespeare's day. The eye still held an outdoor imagery; and in the days when College gates were *really* shut, neither to get in nor out, at eight o'clock, when students read their books under the staircase light, or even by the light of the brazier in the hall, plays were of necessity acted in the daytime.

It was always something of a concession from authority, this acting of plays. Laws against 'masterless vagabonds' included 'Players in their interludes'. Plays were severely censored from their beginning. Subversive political references were suspiciously watched for, both in Tudor and Catholic times. The suggestion of a Playhouse to be built in any neighbourhood called forth protests and petitions against it. Even the famous Globe theatre called forth this protest.

'There is daily, so great resorte of people, and so great multitude of coaches, whereof many are hackney coaches bringing people of all sortes, that sometimes all their streetes

62

cannot contayne them, that they endanger one the other, breake downe stalles, throwe down men's goods from their shoppes, hinder the passage of the inhabitants there, to and from their houses, lett the bringing in of their necessary provisions that the trades-men and shopp-keepers cannot alter their wares, nor the passengers goe to the common water-staires without danger of their lives and lyms, wherebye many tymes quarrels and effusions of blood hath followed etc.'

The early church required an actor to forego his profession before he could be baptised. Companies of players were later required to have a master, often a nobleman, whose livery and badge they wore, and who was responsible for their conduct and the manner of plays they acted, wherever they might wander.

In Queen Mary's reign 1556 there came an order against the Earl of Shrewsbury from the Privy Council for the behaviour of a band of players in the North. Six or seven players 'had named themselves to be servauntes unto Sir Francis Leek and had worn his livery and badge on their sleeves'. Lord Shrewsbury must write to him 'willing him to cause the said players that name themselves his servauntes to be sought for and sent forthwith unto you to be further examined and ordered according to their deserts . . . that he suffer not any of his servants hereafter to goe about the country and use any playes songs or interludes as he will answer for the contrary'. For the absorbing history of the censorship of plays and players in England, Professor Virginia Gildersleeve's book on the subject (from which I quote) is most valuable. The laws against strolling players and the general vagabondage of these companies explains why, when any such appeared in Oxford, they were, like the German bands of our childhood, given money by the Vice-Chancellor to go away again. A definite objection to plays, as such, was sustained. Bodley refused to have them in his Library. 'Haply some plaies may be worth the keeping, but hardly one in forty. For it is not alike in English plaies and others of other nations because they are most esteemed for learning the languages and many of them compiled by men of greate fame for wisdome and learning, which is seeldom or never seene among us. Were it soe againe, that some little profit might be reaped, (which God knows is very little) out of some of our plaie-bookes, the benefit thereof will nothing neere countervaile the harme that the scandle will bring unto the Librarie when it shall be given out that we stuff it full of baggage-books.'

The contempt for players echoes more strongly in Fynes Moryson's judicial mind. He visited the Frankfurt Book Fair and records:
'Germany hath some fewe wandring comeydians more deserving pitty than prayse . . . So far as I remember that when some of our cast despised stage players came out of England into Germany and played at Franckford in the tyme of the Mart, having neither a complete number of actors, nor any good apparell, nor any ornament of the stage, yet the Germans, not understanding a word they sayde, both men and women flocked wonderfully to see their pictures and their actions rather than heare them, speaking English which they understoode not and pronouncing peaces and patches of English players, which myselfe and some English men there present could not heare without

great wearysomeness. Yea, myself coming from Franckford in the company of some cheefe merchants Dutch and Flemish, heard them often bragg of the good market they had made, only condoling that they had not the leisure to heare the English players.'

When kings and queens visited Oxford (and they came often there) there was a great elaboration of play-acting. Queen Elizabeth was so tired with the number of plays which she was required to witness on one visit, that on the next she very skilfully appointed a deputy to attend in her place. But in the case of royal visitors enormous machineries were set in motion. 'A whole kennel of hounds filled the quadrangle of Christ Church while boys shouted from the windows.' On another occasion 'A great tempest was created in which the artificial snow was comfits etc.' and the King's surveyor of works, Inigo Jones, designed the costumes. But these were the entertainments given to princes, not the student-play proper, which at first copied the structure of the moral plays presented by the church.

Sometimes the plays in the hall or garden were classical exercises after the manner of great authors — 'Saturnalia or the origin of Christmas candles'. Discussions by the 'Days of the Week' with Sunday speaking in Latin.

'Now because before were divers youths whose voyces or personages would not suffer to act anything in publicke, yett withall it was thought fitt that in soe publicke a business everyone should do something, therefore a mock play was provided called the "7 Days of the Weeke" which was to be performed by them which could do nothing in earnest — and that they should be sure to spoyle nothing every man's part was sorted to his person and it was resolved that the worse it was done the better it would be liked and so it fell out.'

The impromptu nature of some of the entertainments is evident. 'This showe by our selves was not thought worthy of a stage or scaffoldes, and therefore after supper ye tables were onlye sett together, wch was not done without great toyle and difficulty by reason of ye great multitude of people (wch by ye dorekeepers and divers others, every man bringnge in his friends) had fild ye Hall before wee thought of it. . . .'

'They gave us at ye ende 4 severall and generall plaudites, at ye 2nd whereof ye Canopie wch hunge over the Altare of Fortune (as it had been frightened with ye noise, or meant to signifie that 2 plaudits were as much as it deserved) suddenly fell downe — but it was clenely supported by some of ye standers by till ye company was voyded, yt none but ourselves took notice of it.'

Ingenuity overcame disabilities which seem to have been appreciated by the performers.

Enter a Woman

WOMAN A play without a woman in't
        Is like a face without a nose
        Therefore I come that strife to smite

St. John's Garden Front

Though I have naught to say God knows
And since I can no matter handle
I'll come sometimes to snuffe their candles.

It was later that the countenance of the seniors is admitted with appropriately increased expenditure.

'For X dossen pound of great candells for the plaies at IIIs & IIId a dossen' in 1569 in the Bursar's book of St. John's suggests an interest throughout the college and in 1582 the play has become so fixed an interest that the expenses are shared by the whole College.

'It was granted and concluded and agreed by the President and X seniors that the rest of the charges over and above XXVI li VIIIs & IIIId collected amongst the students towarde the charge of the two tragedyes and a comedy played in the College publickly the XVIIIth XIXth & XX of February 1581 shall be borne by the College and pay'd by the Bursars out of the common coffers.'

'The Bursar's accounts show that the grant from the College amounted to £20 in addition to 20d for Sr. Kite's window broken at the plays and 12d for damage to Mr. Lee's stairs.'

It was when the more ambitious plays of outside authors were attempted by students that criticism became louder. There was the lynx-eye for sedition which was kept on plays whatever party was in power. There was the offence of dressing men in women's garments for the parts of women. There was the character of the plays themselves, such that Milton, himself a contriver and writer of masques, exclaimed with indignation at the sight of students of theology 'writhing and unboning their clergy limbs' in the representation of such female characters who formed the casts of many Restoration Dramas.

The long festivities at Christmas, when students living in distant parts of the country could not go home and settled in to such merriment as they could invent for themselves, gave a real reason for the students' play as an institution and notwithstanding the present day temptation to employ the professional actress too much, as such it remains. All this, however, leads to a caution for the unaware. In all Oxford institutions there is much which *may* be laughed at; much that the undergraduate finds comic and does not scruple to say so; but never, under any provocation must you laugh at the O.U.D.S. You may confess to any cynicism but not this one. The O.U.D.S. is serious. This cheers me greatly and when I read on a play-bill that to disparage the acting of plays 'is no longer fashionable', I am happier still, for Oxford seems so young — young enough to have not yet been completely enmeshed in that elderly self-consciousness which lands the unwary on a slippery slope called by the displeasing modern name of 'Cultural Relations'.

In the year 1948 all Oxford prepared to welcome and show its best to the little Lady born to be its Queen, another Elizabeth. The University of Oxford, the Home of

Learning, can do and produce most things, and for this state visit the O.U.D.S. prepared a Masque. It is some hundreds of years since a Masque was performed in Oxford before a royal person. *Why*, it is difficult to say. Dressing-up and mumming seem so artless a form of entertainment. But in the lean years of today there were no showers of comfits, no elaborate erections of Castles of Plenty. The Gothic College provided the staging. The speakers were 'masked and habited in character'. Hope was the Symbol and a young Princess smiled happily to receive from her hands the thoughts and aspirations of the rising Dawn.

XX

St. John's Christmas Vacation (1607)

The most magnificent and renowned Thomas, by the favour of fortune, Prince of Alba Fortunate, Lord of St. John's, high Regent of the Hall, Duke of St. Giles, Marquis of Magdalene, Landgrave of the Grove, County Palatine of the Cloisters, Chief Bailliff of the Beaumont, High Ruler of Rome, Master of the Manor of Waltham, Gouvernour of Gloster Green.

UNLIKE the long summer vacation which allowed the students time enough at home to help in the harvest, the Christmas vacation was short and was the time for mumming and acting of plays indoors. The College of St. John's has preserved a record of the festivities carried on in the early seventeenth century with many of the plays attempted or produced. It seems to have been a time of great exuberance among the students and of complacence in the University, for we read on one wet dark winter, 'Though the term should have begun on Jan. 11th, the hall was so pestered with scaffolding, that the college allowed them another week to produce another performance'. The election of the Christmas Prince and his court happened as other elections do. It arose from the need of law and order and procedure and is recorded as follows:

'It happed in the year of our Lorde 1607 the 31 October beinge All Sayntes Eve, that at night a fier was made in the Hall of St. John Baptists Colledge in Oxon, accordinge to the custome and statutes of the same place, at wch time the whole companye or moste parte of the studentes of the house mette together to beginne their Christmas. Some came to see Sportes, to witte the Seniors as well Graduates as under-graduates. Others to make Sportes . . . but as it often falleth out, the Freshmen or patients, thinkinge the Poulderlings or agentes too buysie and nimble: they them to dull and backwarde in theyr duty, the standers-by findinge both of them forwarde and violente, the sportes for that night for feare of tumultes were broken up, every man betakynge himself to his reste.'

Unfortunately the night's sleep which was hoped would 'somewhat abate their rage', had only 'sett a greater edge on their furye', and it was evident that if this continued there would be the 'utter annihilatynge of all Christmas sportes for the whole yeare followinge'.

This was obviously impossible, so a controller of the revels was suggested. Thirteen senior Graduates withdrew themselves into the Parlour to debate. Issuing from the parlour they laid hands on a young man for their purpose, but he as vigorously declined the honour. They withdrew to the parlour again. Another determined sally, and the next choice, getting wind of their intention went promptly into hiding and finally to

67

his own room where 'he was in a manner surprised, and more by violence than any will of his owne taken uppe and with continuall and joyfull outcries carried about ye Hall and so backe to his Chamber'.

It was an elaborate affair which was launched. The Christmas Prince had a parliament and swore in loyal subjects. He levied taxes to pay for the merry-makings; sent decrees forth; mulcted the tenants of the College for venison and wine and kept great state, being ceremonially robed and carried to and from his state apartment. An equally elaborate funeral and feast concluded his reign. But though these ceremonies and the drawing-up of coats-of-arms and titles for the members of his parliament would be of absorbing interest to the students taking part they are hardly so entertaining to modern readers. There is an atmosphere of Latin puns and general facetiousness. The students were none of them very old and naive distresses appear in the account.

'It hath beene observed if they which performe much in these kinde of sportes must needs doe something amisse, or at the least such is the daunger and trouble of them, that something in the dooing will miscarry and so bee taken amisse, and such was our fortune at this time; for the Prologue (to the great prejudice of that which followed) was most shamefully out and having but halfe a verse to say, so that by the very sence the audience was able to prompt him in that which followed, yet he could not goe forward, but after long stay and silence, was compelled abruptly to leave the stage, whereupon, beeing to play another parte he was so dasht that hee did nothing well that night.'

'After him Good-wife Spiggott, coming forth before her time was most miserably at a non-plus and made others so also whilst herself staulked in the middest like a great Harry-Lion (as it pleased the audience to terme it) either saying nothing at all or nothing to the purpose.'

With all these troubles threatening the Christmas Prince it is no matter for surprise that S^r. Tucker hid in his room at the prospect of being elected to that eminence. The plays (of which many survive) of this year 1607 in St. John's College were largely topical and some quite charming. *The Dream of the Founder*; *The origin of Christmas Candles*; *The Altar of Fortune*; *The Days of the Week*; *Philomela*; *Narcissus*.

The collapsing of the scenery on top of the players was one minor accident, but there were others more alarming; for 'Periander, going to kill his daughter Eugenia, did not so couch his dagger in his hand but that he prickt her through all her attire'. The stage-manager had manifold troubles. The Prince had 'got such an exceeding cold that he could not bee heard'. The carpenter had not got the stage ready. The actors suddenly remembered, just as they were going on to the stage, that they had not got an epilogue and had to invent one. 'Here wee were all so discouraged that wee could have found it in our hearts to go no further.'

The Lord Treasurer complained to the Prince that his treasury was nigh empty and well it might be, though there were lengthy lists of subscribers and patrons. Young Mr. William Laud, W. Paddy and Mr. Juxon were liberal subscribers. The items of expenditure seem very varied and it was by no means cheap to produce a play even in those days.

Imprimis for 40 dozen of linkes	£4. 10s.
Item for 10 dozen of torches	£4. 10
For dozen of greate waxe tapers	15
For a shute of tawny taffety for the Prince	£4
80 yardes of flannelle for the guardes coates	£5. 6. 8.
For 2 longe women's haires	£2
For fethers, spangles, roses etc.	£1. 10
For 4 thoudsand of pinnes	3s.
For a sett of musitians entertained for 12 days	£5.
To Carpenters for setting up the stage scaffolds twise and for lending boards	£5.

And so on until £63 is reached. No wonder they needed a 'collection'. By such struggles and difficulties our forefathers doubtless became the men they were! But these expensive stagings came at a later time when authority became interested and helpful. There were more elementary affairs in the Hall when 'the plays were clapt together for want of a better' and the stage-scenery was in the Pyramus and Thisbe manner: *The five bells of Magdalen Church* had an artless presentation.

> 'And more for more tuneable proceeding
> I have ta'en down the five bells in our towne
> Which will performe it if you give them heeding
> Most musically though they ring an hour.
> Now I go in to oile my belles and pruin them
> When I come downe, I'll bring them downe and tune them.'

He returns, bringing five other boys tied with bell-ropes, and pulls them one by one, each chanting his own part and so 'ringing the peal'. All simplicity and artlessness itself, one sees, but great fun to the actors and audience.

The thoughts of youth are ambitious and the sum of the plays which the under-graduates of St. John's meant to play and had no time for is a long one. Their titles give some clue to the mind of the undergraduates in 1607. *The Maske of Penelope's Wooers*; *The State of Telemachus*; *The Embassage from Lubber-land*; *The Creation of White Knights of Aristotle's Well*; *Triumph of all the Founders of Oxford Colleges* — this last 'a devise much thought on, but it required more invention and more cost than the time would afford'. It sounds so familiar, all these ingenious thoughts at work, 'making their own fun', and coming up against the hard facts of time and expenditure. They were handsomely helped by their seniors and the Christmas Prince had a stately reign.

It all seemed to go so well that it is something of a shock to read at the end of Sʳ. Tucker's reign (Sʳ. Tucker in later years obtained the third stall in the Cathedral of Bristol; and the chronicler of the proceedings when the 'great fier' was lighted in the hall, Griffin Higgs, became Dean of Lichfield):

'Wee intended in these exercises the practise and audacity of our youth, the creditt and good name of our Colledge, the love and favour of the Universitie, but instead of all these (soe easie a thing it is to be deceived in a good meaning) wee met with peevish-nesse at home, perverseness abroad, contradictions every where, some never thought themselves entreated enough to their own good and creditt, others thought themselves able to doe nothing if they could not thwart and hinder something; moste stood by and gave aime, willing to see much and doe nothing, nay perchaunce they were ready to procure most trouble which would be sure to yield least help.'

The future Dean of Lichfield was a disillusioned man already. No doubt in later life he expected less from his contemporaries as a result of his early experiences as a subject of the Christmas Prince. Yet it was not all disappointing, for Mr. Higgs amends his judgment at the end.

'And yett wee cannot complaine of all. Some ment well and said well, and those took good will for good paiment, good endeavours for good performance,' and surely here is a happy ending:—

'All were so pleased att the whole course of this play [*Periander*] that there were at least eight generall plaudites given in the midst of it in divers places and to divers persons. In the end, they clapped their hands so long, yt they went forth of the colledge clapping.'

St. John's College Mummers

XXI

'Jentacular Confabulations'

Nor were there any fritters at dinner as there used to be;
When laudable old customs die, learning dwindles.

WHEN I, after some years' acquaintance with the City and students of Oxford, now meet a group of these young men (except indirectly the young women do not come under the complaints of their elders here) in an assembly or in the street, I have taken to examining them with gravity and concern. For, in all the reading I have been able to compass, from whatever century and from whatever angle the matter has been regarded, I find one thing very clear, that these undergraduates of Oxford are and always have been 'declining'. The reasons are as many as falling leaves in autumn. From every side these young men are admonished. Sometimes it is the Quakers. In 1653 Mr. Crosfield prays for resignation to God's will in this respect. 'God out of evill can bring good, and why may He not, out of the new Sect of Quakers produce glory to Himself and good to His people if they but with patience wait his leisure.'

At another it is the Coffee Houses which are the root of evil. 'Why doth solid and serious learning decline and few or none follow it now in the University? Answer: Because of the Coffee-Houses where they all spend their time....'

Again it is the decay of old customs (as 'no fritters for dinner') — The gentle Heber writes to a friend (1801) that he had caught a cold by getting up at four o'clock in the morning to see the celebration of the All Soul's Mallard Feast. 'I know not whether you have any similar strange customs in Cambridge, so that perhaps such ceremonies

71

as the All Soul's Mallard, and the Queen's boar's head etc. will strike you as more absurd than they do an Oxford man, but I own I am of opinion that these relics of Gothicism tend very much to keep us in a sound consistent track and that one cause of the declension of foreign Universities was their compliance with such points as these with the variations of manners.'

Dissenters of all ages and sects were, of course, a terrible cause of decline, and in these latter days, worse than all, and still talked of in places with indignant trembling, the admission of women to the University status.

The world is evidently out to shake its head at the University clerk however he trims his course, but the tartest and most acrimonious of complaints comes from a gentleman called Nicholas Mersham. For him, all declensions from moral and stable virtues spring from one cause, 'Jentacular confabulations in the morning'. Unbosoming the soul at breakfast — is for him the horrid cause of the modern moral decline.

Now this perpetually declining undergraduate stretches a long way back into history and to a very early youth. John Evelyn brought his son to Oxford, to Trinity College, at the age of 13. 'He was nearly out of long coats.'[1] Boys who came to Oxford to study (chiefly grammar) began at the age of 10 or 12. They came to the Grammar Schools and some of the early statutes and rulings of the Vice-Chancellor seem to be explained by the very immature youth over whom he had jurisdiction.

In 1465 Thomas Chandler settles a dispute thus: 'Neither of the parties to the quarrel shall abuse or threaten *or make faces at each other*.' Even of the Seniors such rulings as these were considered necessary. 'In the election of a Fellow, morals, learning, and poverty, are the qualifications of the successful candidate. All Fellows must speak Latin. They may not fight, nor use abusive language, nor sing amatory songs nor tell such tales, *nor laugh at each other*.'

1250. 'The gatherings of Masters and scholars to celebrate national festivals in the churches are strictly prohibited and under pain of the greater excommunication they are forbidden to go about dancing in the churches or in the porches disguised with masks or with garlands of flowers or leaves or other materials on their heads.'

The beginnings of the undergraduates were very small — of the Balliol student the early conditions were like this: 'As for the allowance each scholar had (the number of whom was 16) was but 8d. per week, that is a penny every week-day and twopence on Sundays.' The boys were lodged in the many hostels built in Oxford, often by distant monasteries for the students they maintained, who passed in due course to their Bach. and M. Arts degrees. One of the most interesting parts of Worcester College still preserves a row of such hostels, with the arms of the various religious houses which supported each one, above the doors.

The boys and older students came often from distant parts of the country, by road (and indeed, in the usual condition of medieval roads, any journey was a long way).

---

[1] 'Old Mr. Sutton was his schoolfellow and sayd that Lancelot Andrews was a great long boy of 18 years old at least before he went to the university.' *Aubrey's Brief Lives*

They came most frequently in convoy. There were trustworthy carriers of boys called 'Fetchers' who collected them and brought them on horse-back to their various schools and halls. Thomas Traherne arrived at Oxford from Hereford sitting on top of the luggage in the carrier's cart. A very illuminating essay on the early students of Oxford which precedes the first volume of *Munimenta Academica* suggests that one of the most extraordinary differences in the life of medieval Oxford was the influx yearly or oftener of these hundreds of horses. Who, for instance, looked after them? Did Oxford maintain a small army of hostlers and stablemen? To whom did they belong? What became of them? Were they sold, or taken back to the country, and who took them? It suggests a thriving trade in itself, and perhaps the size of the citizens' immemorial grazing-place, Port Meadow, may be explained by this great coming and going twice a year of saddle and pack horses.

The curriculum does not seem to have been very advanced. Books for the children did not exist and the lessons were altogether oral, and in Latin. The Masters of the Grammar Schools 'shall swear that they will be diligent in teaching the boys and disinterested; also that they will attend to their morals. They shall set their scholars copies of verses to compose and also epistles, and they shall be careful to practise them in parsing. They shall teach the boys to construe in English and French, so that the latter language be not forgotten'. Thus, when the teaching was in general oral, the oath to be diligent in teaching was of greater moment than would seem to modern thought necessary, for the learning which the boys came to Oxford to acquire was lodged (for *them*) not in books, but in the heads of their masters and if *they* failed . . . The masters had to collect their own fees from the scholars, and rules both for the safeguarding of scholars from exploitation or bribery of masters by gifts from wealthy undergraduates were found necessary. The ceremony of 'Collections' which has such a different meaning now, both to tutors and to undergraduates, had once a quite exact and literal meaning for both.

The masters seem to have been safeguarded in their turn and their living assured to them, for, to my astonishment, I read: 'When there are no lectures going on in any Faculty he studies, a scholar is bound to attend lectures of the study *most akin to it*. Therefore, as there are no lectures in writing, dictating or speaking French, those who study those subjects or who are occupied in making legal deeds etc. shall attend lectures in rhetoric and grammar, and *shall contribute for the maintainence of Masters lecturing there-in.*'

I was reminded of a small and zealous girl left in charge of a shop, who to my inquiry for a dustpan replied — 'No'm, we haven't any dustpans, but we have some very nice kneeling mats'. Perhaps learning was so highly accounted that so long as you were learning *something* it didn't matter much *what* it was.

There was an unbelievable England around the scholars. 'It came to pass on Monday before the Feast of St. Margaret, that Robert de Lincoln, felon, fled to the church of St. Martin because of the felony that he had committed in slaying John de Cornubia.

The coroners came on that Monday and viewed the said Robert there, and asked him for what course he had fled to the church and kept therein; and there before the coroners he recognized that on the said Monday he slew John de Cornubia feloniously with a knife. The coroners asked him to surrender himself to the peace of the King, but he would not. Wherefore the baillifs were bidden keep good watch lest he escape. Also on Friday after the Feast of St. James the Apostle, the coroner came and asked him to surrender himself to the peace of the King, but he said he would not, and in their presence he abjured the realm, and he received the cross and his port was assigned him at Southampton.' (1346.)

Even in later years there were summary happenings around the University. In 1635 Anthony Wood records 'Extreme cold weather. A poor man died with hunger and cold. He began to die in St. Clement's parish, but the parishoners discovering it, hurried, or rather carried him to the tower in the parish of St. Peter's in the East, to die there, and so save the parish 2 or 3 shillings to bury him'; and 'The law for beggars is that he which last gave him alms, should maintain him if the parish provide not for him where he was born'. The scholars moving within these turbulent surroundings, in spite of certain independence, were subject on two sides to severe rules of behaviour. From *outside* the University came such a statute as this (1572: 14 Eliz. cap. 5): 'All vagabonds unless with a licence are to be whipped and burned through the groulte of the right ear with a hot iron, unless a man of property will be their surety.' Such vagabonds include: 'Unlicenced players, palmists, jugglers, counterfeiters ... *and all scholars of the Universities of Oxford and Cambridge that go about begging, not being authorized under the seal of the said Universities.*'

In 1588 the caution had to be repeated. '*All persons calling themselves scholars, going about begging,* and all seafaring men pretending losses, shall be deemed rogues vagabonds and sturdy beggars.'

(It has been suggested to me, that a generation living on Government grants may have sympathy with those whose public aid was combined with such very free enterprise.)

From *within* the University the penalties were even stricter. 1584: 'No scholars shall sit on bulkes or penniless bench, or other open places, or gadde up and down the streets under paine of imprisonment.' 1636 (Laudian Statute): 'It is enacted that scholars of all conditions, shall keep away from inns, eating-houses, wine-shops and all houses whatever within the city or precinct of the University, wherein wine or any other drink or the Nicotian herb or tobacco is commonly sold. Also if that person does otherwise and is not eighteen years old and not a graduate, *he shall be flogged in public.*'

1666. Four undergraduates who had passed their exam in 1666 were suspended for a year from taking their degrees, '*because they had been convicted of playing at football*'.

Even chess was among the 'noxious, inordinate and unhonest games' expressly forbidden to the scholars of New College by William of Wykeham's statutes. (*Coulton.*)

With such hedges about them the scholars went on from the Grammar School to

Blackwell's

their degrees, often pawning to the various book-chests any article of value they had for the loan of a book from the chests; reading the chained books in the Churches, spending the Christmas vacation in the making and acting of plays, and in the Long Vacation going home to help in the harvest. The bachelors[1] wore boots and the under-graduates pynsons. They were regarded by the townspeople as definitely inferiors.

There seems to be no end to it! Opening the Torrington Diaries, I read John Byng's comment in 1785 — 'Oxford is always gay and the student very impertinent'. Is that the reason why, in official photographs of Oxford streets and colleges, the undergraduate has been carefully tidied away? Not a glimpse of him!

[1] 'Bachelors of Theology may read the Bible, but not as an exercise, in the Long Vacation.' Odd, wasn't it?

Master-Mason

This architecture was not the work of a single class of men, but resulted from the joint efforts of many minds, directing many different tools. High and low, rich and poor, gentle and simple, cultured and uncultured, all combined to the same end, and the authors of the architectural books of the period knew their business when they appealed on their title pages to so many different artificers.

J. A. GOTCH

FROM my window opposite the church of St. Mary Magdalene, I used to watch the old caretaker sweeping the entrance clean for worshippers. After a wedding, the evasive streams of confetti would swirl against the railings like gaily coloured scarves dropped by the wedding guests. On wet days, bus tickets alighted in the alley as if seeking sanctuary. But it was when the big pink chestnut trees shed their weight of leaf and coral blossom that the old lady had a man in to help.

On the pavement and on the old green gravestones the burden fell regularly every year, too heavy for one old woman to sweep away. So the gate would be loosed from its loop and wire and opened for barrow and besom, the gravestones were swept clear and their half obliterated inscriptions were revealed to the sun again and to anyone who had a mind to read them.

It is not often that one is curious enough to enter an old graveyard in a city street. Like certain pictures in certain places, they have been there so long that they are never looked at. They have become part of the furniture of the street. If they were taken away they would be missed, but not for long. The forgotten graveyard is but an open space across which one looks, a shelter of green trees in the open street.

It never occurred to me that anyone of interest might be sleeping under the chestnut trees. The rumble of St. Giles goes on nevertheless where a good 'tradesman' (in the classic old sense) lies, a mason of the days of Laud and the Stuarts, who left substantial evidence of his passage through Oxford upon at least four important buildings in the city. John Jackson, the master-mason, worked for Laud upon the Canterbury Quadrangle of St. John's College, for Nicholas Stone on the porch of St. Mary the Virgin. He was responsible for the Chapel of Brasenose College and the Selden end of Bodley's Library — a considerable contribution to the work of University Building.

It was Michelangelo who said that if one hadn't a good mason one might spare oneself the attempt to build — the master-mason being actually the master tool of more importance even than the material.

In the days of John Jackson, the profession of architect was beginning to emerge as we know it today; that is, of a man withdrawn from the *practice* of building to his study, there to design his great work to the last detail, not only of structure but also of ornament, and to hand over his design to skilled workmen to carry out. So that it is reasonably accurate to speak of Wren's Library or Cockerell's Museum.

But the great early buildings had no such architect. They were things 'not of design but of growth'; works 'which no man intended or foresaw as they now are'. Any great project of building began somewhat after this manner. The client would describe his need. The master of works would draw out a plan strictly for that need (in a church, conforming entirely to the ritual of worship to be followed within) and the multitude of workmen would be collected (sometimes even conscripted) to carry out the work. Much personal freedom was allowed to each craftsman within the set requirements of the work and it is the often incalculable and personal turn given to familar shapes and materials which give the liveliness of the medieval artificer. But the heavy and important part of the work was of course the shaping of stone for building, and the hewers of free-stone became the leaders of the workman, at first in the practical construction and cutting of stone, and then, as education advanced, adding technical knowledge to their practice, being granted degrees with academic robes and a status foreshadowing that of a distinguished architect of today. (A delightful chapter upon the history of the mason is included in Professor Lethaby's *Medieval Art*.)

It is among the type of mason-cum-builder remaining from earlier times rather than that of the later architect that John Jackson appears in the time of Charles I and the Civil War.

The medieval craftsman had his vigorous skill and much scope was allowed to him, but we inherit with these his limitation of knowledge. There was a settled belief, fostered chiefly by Ruskin and Longfellow, that the early builders and workers worked as devout men for the glory of God.

'In the elder days of Art
Builders wrought with greatest care
Each minute and unseen part
For the gods see everywhere.'

But there were not only cathedrals and chantries built. There were beheading-pits and bottle-necked dungeons. There were torture-chambers and ramparts of castles. Were these also begun and ended in prayer? If so, why do curious little entries like this find their way into Oxford account books?

'The little Cloyste begun to be digged and at digging a foundation for ye little lobby, the workmen receive 5s. at several times to make them drink and continue their work longer than ordinary.' Or these cries from the heart of the University in the year 1490?

'The building [St. Mary's Church] is in so tottering a state that people fear to stand near it in windy weather', and in 1493, 'you know how old the building was, and how the Masters and Scholars were often deluged with rain and snow when attending in the Church in rainy weather'.

The inexperience of the early mason was one of the inheritances he left to us, as well as his skill in free-stone.

1655. 'On the Vigil of St. Luke, half of the roof on the south point of the outer chapel joining to the Tower, fell within the Church about nine o'clock that night, and broke all the stones lying on the floor, of which some were ornaments.'

1699. 'This church fell down Mar. 8th when Dr. Henry Aldrich, Dean of Christ Church, designed the present most elegant and noble structure.'

July 31st. 'On Sunday a terrible wind happened in the afternoon while all the people were at Divine Service, and two or three stones and some rough cast stuff were blown from off this tower, which, falling on the leads of the church, a great alarm and outcry was among the people in the church.'

And all this collapsing of structure occurs in a few pages descriptive of early Oxford building. The fact is that we see buildings which survive and have little knowledge of those which fell down or decayed, and since the surviving buildings (mostly of public structures like churches or castles which have had special care taken of their maintenance) are of enduring quality, we have a habit of supposing that all ancient building was so. But old records make it fairly clear that early builders and workmen rose to much the same incentives as they do today, and durable building with better knowledge of engineering seems more probable now than then.

John Jackson, master-mason, with his superior Nicholas Stone, were among the last of the old type of workman-architect-builder to be employed on the Oxford Colleges before there entered with Wren the new study-architect. The name of John Jackson survives in College accounts and litigations and can be traced in connection with the buildings on which he worked.

'Mr. John Jackson to get £20 for his modell of the roof of ye new chappell and his paynes taken about it.'

'To Mr. Jackson 22^{li} which upon a review of the porch and wall at St. Mary's by Mr. Vice-Chancellor (Richard Baylie) and others was judged fit to bee given unto him beyond his bargain (viz 230^{li}) which summe was given by Dr. Morgan Owen for that worke.'

'To Mr. Jackson for making the nest of the King's picture [bust] in the Librarie £6.' Sometimes — and here is a difficulty common both to early and later masons which is seldom taken into account in looking at a great building — he was confronted (as in rebuilding the Chapel of Brasenose College) with a mass of old material of which he is instructed to make use. He is told that the College has, remaining over from the old Chapel (pulled down) a set of perfectly good Gothic windows, a 'good hammer-beame roof', and much worked stone and wood; and he is required to work all these into his new building. An economic fact of this sort, more frequent than is imagined in building and re-building, accounts very often for the medley of architectural styles to be found in any really ancient city. There may be actual need for accommodation. The roof of Jesus College Chapel was designed with open rafters. To accommodate

Catte Street

an apartment above the Chapel, the present lower ceiling was arranged and built and who would suspect an upper story! Economies of other sorts occur; such as are revealed in the alterations now taking place in the Old Schools Quadrangle. Heavy corner blocks of pine-wood are being brought to light. Before the naval building operations in the days of Charles II such blocks were made of English oak. But the extravagant felling of our oak forests for the building of ships caused a scarcity of oak timber and blocks of pine were imported for the building of heavy floored structures. They were imported from Memel and the name of 'memels' sticks to the blocks to this day. The 'means to hand' were often more potent in building decisions than the dreams and designs of architects.

The Gothic had been the accepted English style, used in England with a majesty and beauty seldom equalled elsewhere. But the Renaissance was far advanced in architecture as well as learning. Both styles were used side by side and the new builders often favoured the classic design. It was natural that the College Authorities who had good Gothic material already on their hands, should require it to be used, but John Jackson, being acquainted with the new movement, had his own taste to satisfy. So the anomaly occurred and the classic design of the master-mason's predilection in Brasenose College Chapel, is furnished with a perfectly good set of Gothic windows and other unusual and money-saving features.

It would be an exacting exercise at any time to combine a classic design with a hammer-beam roof and Gothic windows and John Jackson certainly tackled it in an original manner — for he covered his open rafters with fan-vaulting and the result assembled a covering multitude of gilded and ceremonial umbrellas suggestive of splendour even farther East than Rome. His brackets and struts and posts are muffled, reshaped and gilded and the tie-beam appears as a thin rope of gilt. It was a gallant sally and deserved to be supported by posterity, who in subsequent alterations attempted to correct Jackson's flamboyance by an increased severity of decoration elsewhere. It will never be any use. The only way to find peace is to go one better. I remember the problem which faced an acquaintance who had acquired a late-Victorian house with a cast-iron painted and decorated mantelpiece. My host was a man of wit. He searched for something still more of the period, and unearthed a 'hideous' glass case of wax flowers and fruit which he pushed on to the mantelpiece and in an instant he brought everything into harmony. So, in my *Oxford which was never built*, I should have invited the spirit of Bernini to haunt the chapel of B.N.C. Instead of the mortuary slab which is the present altar, he might have raised a baldachino with twisted columns of bronze or set a reredos in low relief supported by two baroque angels. What else? Would he have painted the stalls and set the dumpy little organ on the back of rearing horses? It could never be done! The Baroque was not entertained long in England, though Laud, Stone and Jackson did their best.

The Selden End of Bodley's Library has parallel discrepancies and we find John Jackson finally working on the baroque porch set in front of the perpendicular church of St. Mary the Virgin. Such an addition was also in the movement. Inigo Jones had set a classic front on the Gothic building of old St. Paul's and from the testimony of contemporary prints it looked very well. Such architectural shocks may greet one from time to time in Oxford Colleges. I have even conversed with eighteenth-century amplitude in a room with square-framed windows, only to discover on saying goodbye to my host in the quadrangle outside that the identical windows from without are of an incorrupt Gothic pattern.

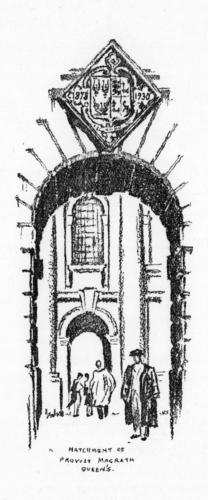

A HATCHMENT OF
PROVOST MAGRATH
QUEEN'S.

XXIII

Baroque in the High

Dr. Harrington condemns it as having no claim to admiration. Dr. Ingram mentions its date, but otherwise ignores it. In 1862 the Oxford dilettanti discussed the advisability of retaining it and only admitted it to have any claims to preservation on account of its historical associations. These considerations prevailed and the porch was not only retained, but extensively restored.

'Aren't those twisted columns rather unusual?' is a question not infrequently asked by earnest people when they look at the Porch of St. Mary in the High St.; and the answer is, 'Yes! in England, where the baroque style never acclimatized itself, and not very frequent abroad, except as an embellishment to an altar, a tomb, a cloister or a pulpit, or any part of a chapel or balcony calling for rich ornamentation.'

The design seems to have been of late pagan use, coming probably from the East. Similar columns were found in the Temple of Clitumnus between Foligno and Spoleto, but they have not been very frequently discovered. The very massiveness of the Roman building precluded much use of what would be an error of architectural judgment. 'The form is not, of course, a fine classical form. It would be impossible in Greece or Republican Rome — but a baroque development in the second-century Empire which seems to have been invented in Asia Minor. It was just the kind of thing that the baroque artists Bernini and Pozzo would like to adopt.'

Bernini, in actual fact, found some ready to his hand, for the largest group of such columns known was in the old basilica of St. Peter's in Rome, forming a kind of ambulatory round the Confessio of St. Peter. They were richly carved with the trailing vine and were known as the *Columns of the Vine-leaves*.

The carefully measured architectural drawings of old St. Peter's made by Fontana — of the Basilica, that is, before it was re-built by Bramante and Michelangelo — show a double row of twelve twisted columns supporting a gallery. Most of these columns were dispersed in the building of the later church, but eight of them are known to have been incorporated by Bernini in the balconies high up under the Dome of St. Peter's. He repeated them in bronze for his baldachino above the high altar and used the design elsewhere — (the church of *Val de Grâce* in Paris). But it was perhaps the fact that the Jesuits adopted the baroque style as their type in their great outburst of church building, that such variations as the twisted columns appear throughout that period in many of the Latin countries, even in South America.

Legends twined about the columns as the vine leaves did. The idea of the reproduction in stone of the twisted tree of the forest can be dismissed as 'poco seria'. A more clinging legend, that the columns in St. Peter's came from Solomon's Temple, lingered through the Middle Ages, having even the solemn approval of Popes. But those were times when anything of an especially rich and ornamental type might be cheerfully baptized, 'From the Temple of Solomon in Jerusalem'. It persisted, however, even in Jewish records, for as late as 1695 there is a Passover Haggadah printed in Amsterdam which shows the entrance to the Holy of Holies supported by two twisted columns with a large isolated one standing outside. But this was probably no more like the Temple in being, than the miniatures of Fouquet who illustrated Josephus. Just as he draws his priests and people in the costume of his own time, so he uses for his background of the ceremonies in the Temple, the design of the most imposing church he knew, which was that of St. Peter's in Rome; and so Herod's Temple in Jerusalem displays the ambulatory of the twisted columns much, one supposes, as they had stood in the original basilica of St. Peter. Josephus himself, who was nearest in date to Herod's Temple, describes the pillars of the actual Temple thus:

'This cloister had pillars that stood in four rows one over against the other all along . . . each pillar was 27 feet with a double spiral at its base. Their chapiters were made with sculptures after the Corinthian order.'

Raphael, in his cartoon of the lame man in the Temple Porch, uses this legend again. His porch before the *Beautiful Gate* is an ample apartment supported by twisted columns decorated with the vine and its tendrils. It may be that such another porch suggested itself to Nicholas Stone the elder. Certainly when Nicholas Stone the younger paid his first visit to Rome one of the first things he did was to visit the Cavaliere Bernini and to copy the work of Raphael. The same Nicholas Stone used the design in a mural tablet in Sonning Church (Berks.). The bombed reredos in St. Paul's Cathedral was supported by twisted pillars. A porch at King's Lynn has similar columns. They add to the variety of plateresque cloisters in Spain. Veronese, following Raphael, uses them in his scriptural subjects. Rubens saw their ornamental value; his

The Porch of St. Mary's

picture of the Earl of Arundel and his wife has a background of twisted columns. A tapestry in Windsor Castle shows them. But on the whole, for building, the varieties of the baroque style never found much following in England. In the sharp religious differences of the time of building the porch of St. Mary's, to favour the baroque style of building with its accessory ornament and figures was to belong to the advanced movement and to be very modern. In the case of Bishop Owen, Laud's chaplain, who built the Porch, it might even be provocative. (The statue of the *crowned* Virgin, emphasizing as it does, a doctrine of the Roman Church rejected by the Reformers, must have given — and it is difficult to see how Dr. Owen could be unaware of such an effect — great offence.)

The Porch, engaging though it is, is really too much of an eyeful for the severe perpendicular church behind it, but it would be a pity, for architectural reasons, to lose this Porch of the headless angels (not beheaded by Cromwell but by the Oxford weather — the photographs of 1850 show them with heads complete) from the Oxford street. When one thinks of what Baroque architecture *can* do when it gets its head, one trembles as at an escape.

The little figure of Mary at present above the door of the Porch remained twenty years without its head. In 1642 (Anthony Wood writes) 'Most of the soldiers (or I thinke all of them) went out of the towne and departed severally, some one way and others another way in severall companies. The London troopers went out about noone and as they came alonge downe the High Streete, Mr. Mayor presented them with wyne at his doore freely; and passinge by St. Marie's church, one of them discharged a brace of bullets at the stone image of our lady over the Church porch, and at one shott strooke of her head and the hed of her Childe which she held in her right arme. Another discharged at the image of our Saviour over All Soul's Gate and would have defaced all the worke there, had it not byn for some townesmen who entreated them to forbeare, they replienge that they had not byn so well entertayned here at Oxford as they expected.' Twenty years later the record reads: 'July 1662. The head of the Virgin Mary set up on her bodie over St. Marie's door and the Babe set up.' Life has many ironies, and it was not its architectural interest but its historical association with Laud which saved the Porch from being demolished in 1862.

The provenance of the porch was, I think, finally decided by Sir Thomas Jackson, R.A., who built the Examination Schools. To him was entrusted the work of examining the fabric of St. Mary's with a view to its safety. Going over the building inch by inch, and its history letter by letter, he has reached these conclusions.

That the design of the porch was by Nicholas Stone the elder, carver to Inigo Jones.

That the work (payments for which are on record) was done by John Jackson the Oxford mason.

That the statue of the Virgin and Child which caused so much trouble was carved by Bromfield and the whole of the work ordered and paid for by Richard Owen, Chaplain to Archbishop Laud.

It was reputed to be John Jackson who took down and hid the figure of the Virgin above the porch in Wadham, where it was replaced at the Restoration. This figure is, of course, like that of the group in Hertford, a statue simply of *Mother and Child,* a presentation which does not seem to have aroused feeling in the same way as the *Crowned Virgin.*

'The whole is a strange mixture of Rococo Renaissance and late Gothic work in unmistakedly English design when closely considered, but resembling at first glance some of the late classic altar-pieces of Belgium.' (*Jackson.*)

XXIV

'A Most Industrious and Excellent Statuary'

17th June 1638. 'I, Hubert Le Sueur, Sculptor, have bargained with the King's Matie of Great Britaine to cast in brasse two statues of 5 footes and 8 inches high. One that representeth our late Souveraine Lord Kinge James, and the other our Souveraine Lord Kinge Charles, for the summe of 340ⁱⁱ of good and lawfull money of England, to be paid in this manner, viz. 170ˡᵇ. beforehand and the other 170ˡᵇ. when the worke shalbe finished and delivered to the surveyor of his Majᵗⁱᵉˢ workes in March ensuinge. And the said Hubert Le Sueur is to receive the afore-said summes without paying any fees for the receipt thereof.' Hubert Le Sueur.
'I was present and witness to the bargain.' Inigo Jones.

THE named sculptors and their works in Oxford are so often, with the exception of Rysbrack and Sir Henry Cheere, in the order of one man, one bust or statue, that to find four fine works with three other attributions to the same man in the possession of the University by one sculptor might reasonably awaken interest.

Hubert Le Sueur, a French sculptor who came to England in the reign of Charles I, finding it a congenial country to work in, and was described by Horace Walpole as 'one of the few we have had that may be called a classic artist', was responsible for the bronze figures of Charles I and Henrietta Maria in the Canterbury Quadrangle of St. John's College, the lordly and authoritative figure of the third Earl of Pembroke, and the bust of Charles I in the Bodleian Gallery.

The age of Le Sueur was the age of foreign artists in England. We had a French queen and a king who was half a Dane, and there were endless exchanges in the arts with the Continent. The general effect left on one by such a book as Walpole's *Anecdotes of Painting* is that of a Court and an England crowded with patrons of every kind of art; the owners of great houses bent on decoration both for interior splendour no less than the embellishment of the great gardens which surrounded them. Ceiling-painters from Holland, statuaries from France and Italy, carvers, portrait-painters, seal-cutters and medallists from other countries, sought the Tom Tiddler's ground of England.

It was not, of course, a new thing to import foreign artists. Torregiano had worked in England. Henry VIII invited Titian, and employed Holbein. Antonio Mor painted Mary Tudor. Van Dyck and Rubens (who was for a time Ambassador to England) were great personages in the Stuart days, and that Le Sueur, a foreigner also, should be the solitary 'classic artist' of the period, known to Horace Walpole, suggests what was indeed rather swiftly becoming the fact, that the prevailing influence in taste had finally set in from elsewhere, retaining a classic bias, but with heavier features, less graceful rectitude of accomplishment. The Low Countries were always nearer to England than Italy and the Italian Classic Renaissance in its clearest expression did not linger long in England. Many influences passed through the Low Countries on their way here, acquiring other features by the way and adding a final English finish. The figure of Nicholas Stone, who studied in Flanders and admired Bernini, and whose name, together with Inigo Jones and Hubert Le Sueur twines in and out of contemporary account-books, is a characteristic figure of the time. Yet again, one reacted upon the other, for we read:

'Van Dyck's portrait of William, 3rd Earl, (Pembroke) was painted not from life, but from the bronze statue of him by Hubert Le Seuur, formerly at Wilton, which stands now in the tower room adjoining the picture-gallery in the Bodleian Library.'[1]

It was also an age of great collecting. Much antique sculpture and ornament was brought from the Continent to embellish English gardens. Rubens himself, with whom a good deal of Flemish influence came into England, was a great collector of classical sculpture. But in spite of this activity of interest in classical remains, the tendency to use more and more mechanically the 'Renaissance box of bricks' was on the way, so that some noticeable upstroke or downstroke of the genuine classic caligraphy must have been apparent in the work of Le Sueur to allow Walpole to call him 'The nearest we have to a classic artist in England'.

The presence of a sculptor trained in the severe Tuscan tradition working successfully and happily in England in that tradition, and acquiring at last the title of Sculptor to his Maj^{tie}, has probably a very simple explanation.

He was two removes from his traditional master John of Bologna. Pietro Tacca, a Florentine sculptor, and first-hand pupil of that austere master of Bologna, was commissioned to finish an equestrian statue in bronze of Henri IV (the father of Henrietta Maria Queen of England) for the Pont Neuf in Paris. The statue was cast in Florence and transported to France, where the young Le Sueur was engaged as assistant to the Italian. The work done in Paris on the statue of the Queen's father might easily draw attention to the young sculptor, and it is suggestive that, when Le Sueur was invited to England from Italy in 1630 by Weston the Lord Chancellor, it was for the purpose of casting an equestrian portrait of Charles I in bronze to stand at the head of the Long Water in Roehampton Park, the Earl's private seat. The model for this statue (which seems never to have been begun before the Civil War drove Le Sueur for a time from England back to France) stands now in Whitehall, Le Sueur's signature on its raised hoof.

The romantic history of this bronze which Gray, the poet, called 'our best statue', has been told many times. Though cast, it was never erected by Le Sueur, but was handed over by Parliamentary authority to a brass-founder of Holborn to be broken up and destroyed. Whether from loyalty to the King, or reluctance to destroy a fine piece of work, John Revett, the brass founder, buried the statue entire, and produced for inspection its equivalent in miscellaneous fragments of bronze. In a similar way the

---

[1] It is interesting that Le Sueur's statue was itself done from a painting by Rubens. This statue, designed originally to stand in the Park at Wilton, has now been placed out of doors in the Old Schools Quadrangle.

Canterbury Quadrangle, St. John's College

statues of Charles and Henrietta in St. John's College, 'were taken from their pedestals in the time of the rebellion and ordered to be sold, but were ignorantly refused because not solid'. (*Rawlison's MSS.*)

At the conclusion of the Civil War Le Sueur returned, as Holbein had done before, to live, work and die in England, leaving a son behind him.

After the age of destruction came the age of re-building. The arts are conservative and even the less wealthy became ambitious of owning portraits. Many of the great Diaries date from this time. The age of the Patron had not yet passed. The Civic statue or group was hardly known. Memorials were still personal, and though the noble patron was often an insolvent and sometimes an arrogant figure, the artist still relied on him. Though the second Charles was a vulgarian in these things, the Court still patronized Art. Unusual discoveries were introduced there and foreign painters still found that, as Rubens discovered, the atmosphere of England was 'not so unsympathetic to Art as its climate would lead one to suppose'.

The diaries of Nicholas Stone and his sons show the extraordinary variety of matters to which a craftsman put his hand in those days of prolific building and beautification, and the 'most industrious and excellent statuary' marched with his generation. Nor were the commissions from great houses to be despised. Nicholas Stone enters in his diary:

'I made 10 mantelpieces for Ser John Woosnam and put them up at Nostall'; and it was with the fashion for decorating gardens with reproductions of famous classic statues and fountains that Le Sueur was engrossed when the Civil War overtook him and drove him from England. Six reproductions of Italian sculptures cast by him were planned to stand in St. James. There was the equestrian statue of King Charles to stand at the head of the Long Water at Roehampton, that of the Earl of Pembroke for the first Court at Wilton, and the fountain at Somerset House, all following the leisured pursuit of beauty so roughly diverted by war.

In 1635 Le Sueur signs himself 'Sculptor to the King', yet one notices that very few commissions were ordered by the King himself, and such an entry as this suggests that there was more honour than emolument in the style of King's Sculptor. 'Yr Ryll Matie is most humbly besought gratiously to give order for the payment of one hundred pounds for a Mercury delivered for her Maties fountain.' Or again:

'30lb. item for yor Maties pourtraite wth the Imperiall crowne wholly guilt, (which piece if it should be neglected or rejected would turn to your poor pet^rs great confusion) what your Matie shall please.' Le Sueur was fortunate enough to have other and more solvent patrons than the king. Among them was Archibishop Laud, President of St. John's College, to whom we owe the bronze figures of King Charles and Henrietta which form the Frontispieces to the Canterbury Quadrangle.

That Le Sueur was a friend of Inigo Jones and possibly employed by him, as our first quotation suggests, that he worked also with Nicholas Stone the master-mason, and that his portraits of Charles and Henrietta form the Frontispieces of the Quadrangle, may have helped the belief that the Colonnades were designed by Inigo Jones. But these bear no authentic trace of the great architect's style and no record of such origin has been found. The commission for the statues was undoubtedly given to Le Sueur by Laud himself.

'From an agreement among the state papers dated 20th March 1633 it appears that Archbishop Laud gave Le Sueur a commission to execute for £400 two bronze statues of the king and queen. These were completed 1634 and presented by Laud to St. John's College.'

It seemed incredible that Archibishop Laud, who arranged the very shoe-ties, so to speak, of the undergraduates, should, in prospect of so munificent a gift from himself to his College, have left it all to a master-mason without any expressed ideas of his own upon the design of the Quadrangle. So that a certain falling into place of contemporary practice in these matters is noted in the recent monograph upon Laud (W. C. Costin), and the statement that Laud himself made a sketch of the cloister which he wished to be designed and built, and gave it to Nicholas Stone, the surveyor of works, to complete and carry out in detail.

The strong presumption that the architectural setting for these figures was designed by Nicholas Stone, master-mason to Inigo Jones, is increased by the knowledge that the actual stone-carvers known to have been employed were the same men employed by Stone for his work on the Gate of the Botanic Garden, and the cloister bears the mark of Flemish Renaissance. Blomfield suggests that the two Frontispieces were designed by Le Sueur. But it would seem to run more like one of the entries in Stone's accounts, that, as 'Blank did the architecture and Stone did the pictures'; so, in this case 'Stone did the architecture and Le Sueur did the pictures'. If Laud, for instance, commissioned the figures first and then had to find an appropriate setting, he would have a precedent in the fountain at Somerset House.

1636. 'Agreed with Gabrell Stacey for the working and setting of the 8 corners of Black Marbell for the sistren at Somersett House for the fountayn in the garden thar (the which he is to work netly) and Robe and set and pin and yont [grout] the joynts *and mak it to agreez with the work of Hubert Le Sueur'* . . . (*Account Book of N. Stone*).

The setting in the case of the Canterbury Quadrangle may have been to frame statues already executed. The double plinth for instance, supporting the columns may have been more than a stylistic variation. It may have been, as in the case of the Fountain at Somerset House 'to make it agree with the work of Hubert Le Sueur'.

What appears to have come straight from Italy and the Classic Renaissance and is very unlike Nicholas Stone or any English sculptor known to the writer, is the setting out of doors of a bronze figure in a stone frontispiece as part of the architectural design. *Stone* figures are so used — those of Nicholas and Dorothy Wadham at Wadham, for instance — but *bronze* figures so used seem to be confined to those of Hubert Le Sueur in St. John's College.

John of Bologna (in whose tradition by way of Pietro Tacca Le Sueur worked) and

Donatello set such bronze figures in architectural designs out of doors in Italy, but it is unfamiliar in England. Le Sueur's treatment of his figures recalls his Italian masters. The presentation of Royal personages to be accommodated as perpetual ornament in architectural niches carries the Renaissance tradition. The eyeless complaisance of Charles, to lend dignity to an insignificant stature, and the shrewish pride of carriage of Henrietta have a certain romanticism which may be French, but the seizing first of an idea rather than a realism is the conventional Renaissance approach. Later, Le Sueur was to complete a finer figure with greater ease and grace, that of the third Earl of Pembroke, Chancellor of the University. From Rubens who made the sketch for this figure (a bronze statue to be seen at low altitude in the round) Le Sueur had learnt a great deal. The freer and more sumptuous treatment of the figure may have been due to Rubens's flowing line, or to the ripening of Le Sueur's knowledge.

XXV

A Rage of Rain

IT may be that a sudden flight of swans in front of the darkened towers of Oxford foretold rain as the country people said it did. The outstretched white skein spun, circled widely and then dropped. The evening sky, so turbulent and charged with rain, launched a sudden savage arrow of light upon the towers huddled and crouching in the valley, and a rainbow lit swiftly upon the ruffled sky.

'These low meadows are often overflowed with a rage of rain' wrote Leland centuries ago; and now in a night the rage of rain has fallen. The dawn, which is only known to the fields and their softly-awaking life is grey with a lift, and in the South a coolness of rain. It breaks on dim flood-water, rising foot by foot, until it flows between the Hinksey hill-side and the grey towers of Oxford like a river Ganges.

Last night the elm trees were a burning orange; the rainbow triumphant! Oxford, which yesterday was without shadows, like a city nailed to a black sky, today has reflections. The flood-water, wan, but stilled and magical with the reflections of waiting awakening spires, gives to Oxford the appearance of a port, with the red-roofed field-barns like strange arks making for the unfamiliar haven. The tops of the drowned willows gleam like the buoys of a tidal channel and there is a shudder of green in the silver flood where the grass grows on high ground. Instead of cattle walking there are reflections and simulated towers. The inland city takes on the semblance of Venice rising from the sea.

It was from the hills above Hinksey that the students of Mr. Hearne's day used to take their walks to 'see the views'. The modern views would astonish them in some

Flooded Meadows from Ferry Hinksey

matters. Incandescent Oxford of the strange flood-lighting invention would have seemed
to them miraculous, but not the strange Port of Oxford, riding harbour-lights across
the flood the water gleaming beneath her walls and the lamps striking down through
the unfamiliar element in a tremulous search for her familiar green meadows.

XXVI

'I'm Going to Sweep Cobwebs from the Sky'

Hangs there not in heaven's vault some prodigy seen by Austrian eyes and Austrian spy-glasses; in the similitude of an enormous wind-bag? By Heaven! answer spy-glasses, it is a Montgolfiere, a balloon, and they are making signals! Austrian cannon-battery barks at this Montgolfiere, harmless as a dog at the moon.   Carlyle.

THERE must be a time when the beautiful tower of St. Peter in the East is in shadow, but it seems to happen that I always pass that way when it stands favoured of sunshine, making a perfect architectural composition of the narrow medieval street. So, though it is in reality rather a dark church, I call it for my private aesthetic satisfaction St. Peter's in the Light. (It is chronicled as S. Petrus in Oriente.) It is said to be the first church built of stone in Oxford. It stands, as a church *should* stand, noticeable, yet withdrawn. Its deep crypt was for seven years, appropriately enough, a shelter from air-enmity, for at its entrance is a head-stone, and on its interior wall a tablet which marks that there is buried in the churchyard a quiet man called James Sadler, a pastry-cook who was for a moment the most famous man in England, and but for his retiring habit of wishing to perform his feats in private without acclamation, might have been on a certain day one of the most famous men in the world. For he was the first Englishman to make a balloon ascent and he did it in Oxford, from the top of Headington Hill three days before Lunardi ascended, to the thrill and applause of all England. Lunardi's ascent was on September 15th, 1784.

'England was again unfortunate in that the honour of bearing the imposing title, "First aerial traveller in Britain" should have fallen to a foreigner, because, only three days before Lunardi's flight, a Mr. Sadler, an Englishman, essayed a flight in a Mont-golfière balloon. Not being a publicist, he repaired to a quiet spot in the country, Shotover Hill in Oxford, in order to make the experiment. Unhappily the balloon caught fire as it left the earth and although Mr. Sadler escaped from the conflagration, his attempt can only be regarded as a failure. A few days after Lunardi's flight he tried again and was successful, for he flew fourteen miles, from Oxford to Hartwelle near Aylesbury. Unfortunately his opportunity for becoming the first aerial traveller in England had passed.' (*Some Milestones in Aviation: W. E. Johns.*) He still, however, re-mained the first *Englishman* to ascend, for Lunardi, though he made his flight in England in 1784, was Italian. To a young generation who have never known and perhaps cannot imagine the world without electricity, or gas put to any other use than lighting, a genera-tion which objected in turn to fixed and fitted baths, gas-stoves, public steam laundries and the 'awkward' look of motor cars must appear ludicrous. Yet as a cautionary tale against ridicule and as an amusing contrast to the stupendous ease with which the Royal Air Force move about the sky on their wings, here is a military problem (or its solution) presented to a sceptical War Office by a ballooning ace, years ago. 'The present condition of war with Mexico will require our forces to reduce Vera Cruz. I will therefore suggest a plan to our War Department, which will render the capture of the Castle of San Juan de Ulloa as feasible and easy as the launching of a frigate. Although the plan I shall propose may seem novel to many, still a brief detail of it, I think, will satisfy the most credulous of its efficiency. In the first place it will require a balloon of common twilled muslin of about 100 feet in diameter. This machine, properly coated with varnish, will retain its buoyancy for many days and weeks. It will be capable, when inflated, to raise over 30,000 lbs. say 20,000 independent of its own weight, net-work, car and cable. It can be inflated in a day, or less time if necessary. The process of inflation can be accomplished on land, or on board a man-of-war at sea, as circumstances may require. The car to be laden with percussioned bombshells and torpedoes to the amount of 18,000 lbs. which will leave 2,000 lbs. for ballast and men. Thus it will be ready to be placed in position for action in a very short time. The cable by which it is to be manœuvred may be at least five miles long, so that the balloon at a mile of elevation would leave the vessel or land position which acts as a retaining point out of reach of the castle guns and under cover of our own batteries. The man-of-war balloon, hovering a mile above the castle like a cloud of destruction would be entirely out of danger of the enemies' guns, since they could not be made to bear on an object immediately above them. The position of the balloon as to height and distance from the retaining point could be maintained by keeping a proper eye to the ballasting. As it would become lightened by the discharging of shells and torpedoes, an adequate quantity of gas can also be discharged. With this aerial warship hanging a mile above the port, supplied with a thousand percussioned bombshells, the castle of Vera Cruz could be taken without the loss of a single life to our army, and at an expense that would be comparatively nothing to what it will be to take it by the common mode of attack.' (*John Wise*.) The reception of this scheme was not cordial.

'At a recent party in Frankfort, Ky, the subject [of taking San Juan de Ulloa by balloon] became a topic of conversation. After a number of persons had said their say, pro and con, a distinguished wit — an ex-governor of the State — was called upon for his views touching the same. With great dignity he pronounced the plan an admirable one, and the inventor a man of military genius, but, he added, I think it will be a very troublesome matter to enlist volunteers for that service.'

The longing to sail the skies has always hovered as a will-o-the-wisp before the eyes of mankind, and more and longer ingenuity has been directed to the mastery of the air throughout the history of the world than is imagined, from the Chinese kites to Jet Propulsion. It came at last, that inflated bag — a fire balloon which could sail the air alone in the presence of thousands. Then, greatly daring — a sheep, a duck and a goat were sent like the experimental dove from Noah's Ark, and came down undamaged. Louis XIV suggested a voyage by criminals — until at last inventors dared to go themselves and among them Mr. Sadler of Oxford with his friend Mr. Windham as passenger. An 'ingenious' gentleman Mr. Sadler, for in the making of the balloon in which he ascended from Shotover Hill he was 'the sole projector, architect, workman and chemist'. A little later he was to have all the publicity which a growing interest could give him, for, 'in the presence of a great multitude', with military bands playing, and with the Duchess of Richmond presenting his flag, this quietly persistent gentleman set out from Ireland to fly the Irish Sea. He got on so well that on approaching the Isle of Man he saw no reason why Liverpool should not be included in his journey. Alas, the winds in the lower atmosphere were contrary and blew him away to sea again where he was obliged to deflate his balloon and his ambition and come down near the first ships he could see. The sailors were so alarmed at the flop in the water of the great bag with its ropes, and the tackle, so liable to become entangled in their own rigging, filled them with such terror, that they prepared to make off. Poor Mr. Sadler with his balloon tearing at a great pace through the water besought them to run the bowsprit through the silken bag and so reduce its danger. They at last did this and the fishermen of Morecambe Bay dragged the exhausted aeronaut aboard just in time. It was left to his son Windham (christened after the friend who ventured with him in his early flights) to achieve the first crossing of the Irish Sea.

There was publicity in plenty for Mr. Sadler in later years. There are coloured prints showing his 'aerial voyage' to Tilbury, Mr. Garrick presented him with a snuff box, and on November 12th, 1784, he 'ascended in an inflammable air-balloon from the Physick Garden in Oxford in presence of a surprising number of people of all ranks, and the Lord Chancellor, Lord Grenville. The balloon being sufficiently filled by a little before one o'clock, Mr. Sadler placed himself in the boat which was fastened by ropes to the net which went over the balloon. Then the machine, being abandoned to the air, ascended with such velocity, that in three minutes time it was hid in the clouds, but a few moments after became visible again; and thus it appeared and disappeared three or four times, seeming always to ascend and at the same time moving with great rapidity in the direction of the wind which blew rather hard from the Sea. In this voyage Mr. Sadler crossed Otmoor and Thame and other places, but an aperture made in the balloon almost as soon as it was launched exhausting the inflammable air very fast, obliged him to throw out successively all his ballast, provisions, instruments, etc. and at last forced him to descend at Hartwell near Aylesbury which is about 14 miles from Oxford, which length he travelled in 17 minutes, so that he went at the rate of nearly 50 miles an hour'. It was by such tedious and painful processes men aimed to reach the stars, and not by any means with the full approval of their fellows.

In 1864 *Blackwood's Magazine* has this paragraph:
'Next to these (Alpine climbers) in order of utter uselessness are the people who go up in balloons, and who come down to tell us of the temperature, the air-currents, the

The Broad from the Sheldonian

shapes of clouds and amount of atmosphere pressure in a region where nobody wants to go, nor has the slightest interest to hear about.'

The facetious were even more ready. The benefits of ballooning were counted jocularly as one is instructed to count one's blessings. They suggested — A Balloon to light all England, by fixing it at such an elevation as to enable a strong and piercing light to illuminate the country round, from Lands End to John O'Groats.

A balloon with which to discover new countries by passing over hitherto inaccessible boundaries.

A balloon with a large reflector and burning glass to bring a little summer heat at Christmas time.

A balloon for delicate constitutions to change its position according to the exact climate required.

A balloon to distribute advertisements all over the world.

A balloon for Pre-Raphaelite artists, by which they may travel up close to the wonderful effects they are so fond of.

A balloon for people who want to keep out of the way, and a detective balloon by which the policeman can look down other people's chimneys and through other people's sky-lights and so find out 'all about it'.

Horace Walpole amused himself and in the light of later developments was funnier than he had any intention of being. He writes in 1784:

'But I chiefly amused myself with ideas of the change that would be made in the world by the substitution of balloons for ships. I supposed our seaports to become deserted villages, and Salisbury Plain, Newmarket Heath (another canvass for alteration of ideas) and all Downs (but *the* Downs) arising into dockyards for aerial vessels. Such a field would be ample in furnishing new speculations. But to come to my ship news! The good balloon, Daedalus, Captain Wingate, will fly in a few days for China. He will stop at the Monument to take passengers.

'Arrived at Brand-Sands the Vulture, Captain Nabob; the Tortoise now from Lapland; the Pet-en-l'air from Versailles; the Dreadnought from Mount Etna, Sir W. Hamilton commander; the Tympany, Montgolfier, foundered in a hurricane. The Bird of Paradise from Mt. Ararat; the Bubble, Sheldon, took fire and was burnt to her gallery and the Phoenix is to be cut down to a second rate. In these days old Sarum will again be a town and have horses in it. There will be fights in the air with bows and arrows, and there will be a prodigious increase of land for tillage, especially in France, by breaking up all public roads as useless.' *If he'd only known!*

Was it possible that Oxford wits could leave this startling innovation alone, seeing that the world was in two minds about the events happening in their city? Not a bit of it! There is a delightful picture of Mr. Warton (Thomas) deciding to make an ascent (without Joseph) to write an ode to his Sovereign one mile above the earth. He therefore 'repaired to Christ Church meadow, with my ballast, provisions, cat and speaking trumpet'.

95

The pastry-cook who had invented the balloon had also provided Mr. Warton's luncheon.

'A small pot of prunes, a half of a plain diet bread and cake ... a loaf of sandwiches, three bottles of old ale, a pint of brandy, a sallad ready mixed, a roll of collar'd eels, a cold goose, six damson tartlets, a few China oranges, and a roasted pig of the Chinese breed.'

'Alas,' (says the wit) 'my ascension was majestic to an uncommon degree of tardiness.'

The machine had to be lightened before Mr. Warton could write his ode. He sacrificed his ballast. 'My own History of Poetry, my late edition of Milton's Minora, my miscellaneous verses, odes, sonnets, elegies, Inscriptions, Monodies and Complaints. My observations on Spenser, the King's last speech, and Lord Montmorres's pamphlet on the Irish revolutions. On throwing out his Lordship's Essay, the balloon sprung up surprisingly.'

The naughty satirist allows Mr. Warton to finish his ode to his Sovereign (after again lightening the Balloon by throwing out all that remained imprinted of his own poems) and brings him down on a Church weathercock with nothing but his Majesty's speech, one pen, the paper of his ode and a small ink-bottle!

'After the month of February, balloons of both kinds, but especially those filled with rarefied air, became very common in England as in other parts of Europe. In London during the Spring, the Summer, and the Autumn, paper balloons, raised by means of splints of wire and generally from 3 to 5 feet in diameter, were seen flying by night as well as by day. All ranks of people seem to have found pleasure in such kinds of experiments, and so much had the subject engaged general attention, that, both in earnest and in jest the epithet of balloon was annexed to articles of dress, of house furniture, of instruments etc. Thus one commonly heard of balloon hats, balloon colours, balloon coaches, and such-like empty phrases.' So it turned out that Mr. Sadler with his turn for privacy in investigation became in the movement. Oxford seems now and again to have backed a *winning* and not a losing cause, and as the formidable modern device for riding the winds circles over the alert population for their defence and guard, quiet James Sadler, 'the first Englishman to ascend the skies', sleeps at peace in St. Peter's Churchyard, and a public-house in a back street called the *Air-balloon* is all that remains of the excitements.

XXVII

'All the Fair Series of the Whiskered Race!'

And there finding a plenty of good pictures, God forgive me, how my mind ran upon them, and bought a little one for my wife's closet and concluded presently by buying £10 worth.

PEPYS

Some people hang portraits up
In a room where they dine or sup.

BROWNING

WHAT unwritten social law has arranged that we dine with our ancestors it is not my purpose to trace. (Portraits of Kings used to decorate living-rooms as early as 1322.) A dining-room apparently, failing a picture gallery in the grand manner, is the proper lodging for family portraits, unless, indeed, the staircase and landings are added to the hanging space. In the monastic order which preceded that of the residential college, the over-docile young men ate their meals to the reading aloud of cautionary tales and passages from the Fathers. Do the College ancestors, mute upon the walls of their Hall, serve to the undergraduate of today this dual purpose? Perhaps as in the case of Mrs. Primrose it is to 'put them in mind of their end' (not their mortal end, as in the case of Goldsmith's Vicar's wife, but of the end of their ambition) that the College Portraits raise benign countenances upon the youth at the Hall tables, and since to most diners the portraits are part of the furniture, let us bring them out of the shade a little, for the cloud of witnesses in Oxford is an important and increasing part of the Oxford man's inheritance.

Once, in a fine but little-visited Ayuntamiento in Spain, we were taken round the

Alcalde's portrait-gallery by a dignified but uninstructed official. To our garrulity on the portrait originals he had one unimpeachable reply. 'Claro! Sono personajes!' ('It is evident! They are personages.') A courteous Librarian of Cambridge University once spent a valuable morning showing us the treasures of his library. In a lighter interlude we were shown the bust of a man standing on a table in an alcove. The inscription on the plinth was covered by a book propped in front. We were made to guess the name and origin. Even the cleverest of us only got as far as 'It *might* be', when, by a swift tap the book fell down and disclosed the inscription 'SMITH'. It *might* be!

Every College Hall, Library and Common Room has its own portraits. Christ Church has now three picture galleries. Special portraits are sometimes sought out with the occasional disillusioned comment 'So *that's* what he looked like!' but in the main they hang between heaven and earth as little regarded as the timbers of the roof. Sometimes one can say, as of Orchardson's portrait of Bishop Francis Paget, 'His best portrait'. Sometimes the portraits look as though they had been frankly deserted by their owners and hidden in a College in so conspicuous a place that like 'The purloined letter' no one notices them.

Three exhibitions of historical portraits held in Oxford some years ago produced admirable and detailed catalogues by Mr. C. F. Bell which formed the basis of further labours by Mrs. Reginald Lane Poole in her three volumes of *Oxford Historical Portraits*. This remains the book of reference for years to come and is invaluable in visiting the College and University galleries; though a number of later additions have been made to the collections.

There are many ways of approaching a gallery of portraits. Not everyone can spend so entertaining a morning as a famous old Italian model, whose method of inspecting portraits was to wander round, pointing out for which part of a famous portrait he himself furnished the limbs or sat for the robes. But it is a pleasant way of re-animating Oxford to inquire into its personalities. Unexpected crumbs of knowledge fall in one's path. Tracking down the origin of the busts on the Janiculum in Rome once gave me a great pleasure in early Italian history.

Here is the satisfied complexion of Thomas Gaisford, Regius Professor of Greek — 'You will never be a gentleman,' said the great Dean to this undergraduate with lordly candour, 'but you may succeed with certainty as a scholar. Take some little-known Greek Author, and throw your knowledge into editing it. That will found your reputation.' So! So! That is what Greek professors have to put up with in their youth, and there hangs Pickersgill's portrait of Thomas Gaisford, Regius Professor of Greek, and *sticker-in*!

The great men of your early admiration you seek in their own colleges and wonder at their wigs and catch at last the noble aspect of your great one beneath an unfamiliar headdress or surmounting a ruff. You may search, not for sitters however eminent, but for painters, and be rewarded by a combining of both — Millais's portrait of Gladstone. Joannes Corvus of Richard Foxe, Orchardson's portrait of Paget, Romney's

Christ Church Hall

of John Wesley. Reynold's of Dr. Johnson, Gainsborough, Zoffany. (Among the moderns, save for a pencil portrait, there is the notable omission of Sargent.) In very early painted portraits the sitter, who was also the donor, appeared in a humbly kneeling attitude in the company of the Saint whose was the real picture. Portrait-painting was not greatly followed in England until Tudor times.

Nevertheless it is the iconography of the pictures for which they were painted. One looks first for likeness and secondly for the painter. For the painting of the great there were recipes. Your emblems were as important as yourself and you must be made to conform to the accepted attitude and expression. Early Italian and Byzantine books on painting are entirely explicit on these matters. So that the early portraits are of the authority rather than the person; the portrait-painter being of the status of trades or craftsmen painting portraits to recipe. One does not know whether such pictures are like the people or not. The dignity and the robe are stressed — there is the pose and gesture of authority, the uplifted hand, the jewels and robes of office.

From this 'Head of the House' period, stylized and formal, through the great Tudor and Flemish periods, through the declining period of the Restoration with Lely and Kneller as its prophets, through the eighteenth century with Gainsborough and Sir Joshua, the consciousness of the art of portrait-painting grows, and a great man poses as a conscious great man for posterity, until finally the Conversation Piece, revived of late years, seems bent on edging out both portrait and painter for the substitution of a piece of furniture for the wall. In the modern Conversation Piece, a sophisticated negligence of pose is sought, as if the sitters raise their heads from port or dessert to notice the entrance of the painter — '*That* fellow!' There is, however, one safeguard for posterity in the group-painting of Fellows — Fantasies in taste are spared to us. No gentleman preparing to be painted as one of a group in the Common Room is likely to have the temerity to suggest that he pose in a toga; nor are any three members of a College (Trinity) likely to arrange themselves on a background of Old Castile as Don Quixote, Sancho Panza and the Porter!

Beware then of the Conversation Piece for it opens the return to the primitive recipe-books of painting, as if the Hermenaia of Mt. Athos were to be re-named that of Oxford; or a latter-day Cennino Cennini be given his head, issuing to attentive craftsmen precise rules for the painting of eminent persons in company, a manner of painting so stylized, that, though every eminent person looks much like another, a confident nobility of aspect prevails. The instructions to the modern painter of the Conversation Piece might run something like this:

'For the gray hair of an older professor use usta mixed with white and cause the hair to cover the head smoothly and in no way rumpled; for the gray hair does not alone signify old age, but the veneration attached to an advanced condition of learning.' Or —

'In every College there are curious and antique practices and these are better portrayed by the painting of the Junior Dons lest levity arise on account of the Seniors. At the mixing of the bowl of milk-punch in the College of St. John the Baptist, the youth of the Fellow handling the liquor should be stressed. Carmine (shaded towards the ear) should colour the cheek, and the hair be golden to signify youthfulness. Hilarity may be conveyed by a marmoset on the shoulder, but should be painted less than life-size, lest the mommet be considered mistakenly to be of the company.'

The problem of the portrait-painter confronted with his sitter is an immediate one. Exactly how should a distinguished scholar or benefactor be called upon to adorn the walls of his College? 'Coleridge was an exquisite poet for a few years, an eminent owl for a lifetime!' Suppose the portrait-painter, dreaming of the 'exquisite poet' should after all be confronted with the 'eminent owl'. And again in what manner should the presentation be made? John Donne had a fancy to be sculptured in his shroud and I have seen a photograph of Miss Edith Sitwell lying in a coffin with pointed Gothic hands: but this mode did not seem to attract and was not resumed. There are dignity, propriety and (more often than seems likely) affection to be considered. Is the sitter to be perpetuated with the easy informality of the natural man as in Francis Dodd's portrait of A. L. Smith, Master of Balliol, or Nicolson's portrait of Saintsbury, and Moynihan's H. W. Garrod at Merton, or must the robe perpetually overawe?

It hardly seems fair to be so impressive and important that you put a perfectly blameless undergraduate off his dinner! So that he's going to change his place at table. He isn't going to sit opposite that old Bishop any longer! Four feet of eminence is to be made to fit into a gold frame and look down on a young generation who will presently ask who he was. It is perhaps, part of the penalty of distinction that a portrait is often painted too late, when the sitter is possibly weary of his own fame and certainly of the painter. The character of a face may become more defined in age, but it may also be far withdrawn, and nothing astonishes a painter more than the extraordinary lack of observation people give to the faces of their intimate friends. Having familiar acquaintance, familiarity with features is assumed. 'Why, that isn't the least like So and So! He has a delicate aquiline nose, and wonderful hair!' Possibly so, twenty years ago, which is the last occasion (probably on making acquaintance) that the critic really looked at the sitter. But in twenty years the nose may thicken in outline, and hair fade to grey, and that is what the painter sees now. No College cares to spend money on uncertain futures. There is, it is true, Swinburne's boyish red head, but that particular portrait was presented, not commissioned.

To the undergraduate the assembly of the mighty dead is august enough to disconcert, but take them one by one (for, after all, they *lived* one by one) and they become even friendly in aspect. Does the heart of this generation feel no throb when it reads: 'Robert Conny, Physician to the wounded landed at Deal 1692' or learns the heart-warming fact that 'Thomas Allen (Trinity) was the soul and sun of all the mathematicians of his time'; or discuss the twang of malice describing William Lancaster (Queens) as 'Old Smoothboots who has done so much mischief in the University'? From Mr. Bell's Catalogue he may learn a multitude of enlightening facts and even be admonished; for 'John Prideaux of Exeter, 1578-1650 [who became a Bishop] did servile offices in the kitchen, the while he minded his book'; and Joseph Hall, 'a rope-dancer and an acrobat, exhibited his skill in the streets of London'.

The 'Mother George', the scullion of Christ Church, 'Thomas Hodges, servant to the chaplains room', the 'Giant of Brasenose', are specimens of what a great growth like a University carries happily along with it; patronage and jokes, democracy and friendly liking, the pleasant affections and humanities of Oxford not only the seat of learning but the Mother Beloved. Even a grim portrayal like the undergraduate's 'old Bishop' may have a gentler side. There is a portrait of Dean Nowell, 'hands holding a fishing-hook; other fishing-hooks on a table, a fishing-rod resting upon pegs against a wall'. There is only a dim art-import in the portrait of Galileo, but the affection of his disciple and first biographer Viviani who sent it as a present to Oxford gently illumines it for us.

Of the shocking uses to which portraits may be put, one must instance the painting which became a punctilio between two opposing political factions. When the one party entered the room and found the face of the portrait regarding the spectators they promptly turned its face to the wall; when the other faction entered, they as promptly turned it back again.

There are curious lapses in the Collection. It is strange that Oxford, which has had such close intercourse with foreigners in matters of learning and music, should have none of the great foreigners among its portrait-painters. (In the matter of sculptured portraits the University has fared better.) There is no original Van Dyck of Laud even at St. John's College, which he did so much to enrich. Christ Church has no Holbein portrait of Cardinal Wolsey or Henry VIII, and though Rubens drew the figure of the E. of Pembroke for Le Sueur there is no portrait by him in the galleries. There is no Antonio Mor. Spasmodic attempts to make a 'Series' of certain portraits presume some kind of collector and there have been such, interested more in the capturing of any sort of canvas to complete or round off a series than in the excellence of the painting. There was once and once only a Mayor of Oxford who was an artist, in the seventeenth century. His name was John Taylor and he was commissioned to make a series of portraits of the Founders of Oxford Colleges. Alas! these, painstaking though they were, were shed by their Colleges and hung in the old School's gallery. There have been series of astronomers, of doctors, of queens and musicians, the last the most interesting because the most intelligent and complete — 39 portraits collected by the Dr. Heath who founded the Music Lecture and Library in 1626. But the enthusiasm of one generation may flag in the succeeding one. A series may be dispersed or displaced until someone flames with a like enthusiasm and fetches them out of their dark corners again. A more interesting series might be a succession of portraits by one painter, and this Oxford possesses in the fifteen small pastel portraits by Lewis Vaslet at Merton. (Two more by this painter, of interest to St. John's College, have recently been acquired by its President.) Christ Church has nine portraits by Kneller.

The series of Chancellors' portraits begins at the Restoration; that of the Founders in the sixteenth century. The Tradescants (probably by John de Critz) hang in the Ashmole Gallery.

Those who have themselves adorned and embellished Oxford — the great architects — have, in their turn, been nobly commemorated. A superb bust of Christopher Wren by Edward Pierce and a fine one of that strange Chancellor, Oliver Cromwell, stand in the Ashmolean. There is a good bust of Nicolas Hawksmoor (said to be the work of Sir Henry Cheere) in the buttery of All Souls. There is Nash by Lawrence at Jesus College, and a capital stout old Sir Robert Taylor waving his plans in the Taylorian building.

There is, alas, no Hogarth; but when English portraiture improved so suddenly and so definitely in the eighteenth century, there came into existence here a fine crop of Reynolds and Romneys (chiefly at Christ Church) though the shyer and greater Gainsborough is not well represented by his two portraits. It is appropriate that Kneller should have presented his own portrait to the University. It is housed in the Bodleian.

Corpus Christi has the noble early sixteenth-century portrait of its Founder, the Bishop Richard Fox by Joannes Corvus, the finest Founder's portrait in Oxford. Of the same high order of early portraits is the Anne of Cleves in the President's Lodging at St. John's. This portrait was the gift of their Fellow, Dr. Rawlinson, who gave 40 or 50 portraits to Oxford and who died in 1757.

Pembroke has all that is wanted in its portrait of Samuel Johnson by Joshua Reynolds. In Balliol the portrait of Robert Browning by his son should not be overlooked; and a small painting of Swinburne by W. Bell Scott is there also. Exeter possesses a Lewis Vaslet portrait of that great benefactor to the National Gallery the Rev. W. Holwell Carr; but a copy of a medallion is all that represents John Ruskin at Corpus Christi.

The oddest early portrait of a Founder is that of Walter de Stapleton painted and presented by the lively Rev. W. Peters, R.A. For the thirteenth-century costume the artist has gone, Mrs. Lane Poole tells us, to the picture of Bossuet by Rigaud in the Louvre. Trinity has a good early portrait of its Founder, Sir Thomas Pope, and a treasure in the Reynolds portrait of Thomas Warton in its Common Room. St. John's has a number of interesting portraits in the President's Lodging — the Anne of Cleves and the Founder, Sir Thomas White — but no Van Dyck portrait of Laud. There are other sound old pictures here like the John Case with the little skeleton before him, but the best works of art at St. John's are the Le Sueur statues of Charles I and his Queen with which Laud enriched his new cloister.

Jesus has an early picture of one Founder, Hugh Price, and a half-length panel of its Co-Founder, Queen Elizabeth, in its Common Room. In the Warden's Lodgings at Wadham hang two good early portraits of Nicholas and Dorothy Wadham, the Founders; and that fine pious portrait of Phillip Bisse who founded the College Library and died in 1613. Of this portrait Anthony Wood notes that, in memory of Dr. Bisse's gift to the Library, 'The Foundress caused his picture to be drawn from head to foot with his doctoral formalities on and to be hung over the door of the Library'.

Eights Week: From Christ Church Boat House

The wheel has revolved and in the painting of modern portraits for posterity the shedding of all 'doctoral formalities' is imminent. The 'common man', the jannock, bed-rock individual behind the trappings of learning, the man who lives and dies like other men, and, like them, smokes a pipe, overshadows us. From here two paths diverge. A succeeding generation may demand to be painted in silk-velvet and moon-stones. We may, on the other hand, be furnished with our great men, as it were, by suggestion; their ideas and accomplishments arranged on plates, their eyes all round their heads, so that you can 'sink the original and not hurt the picture'. But what of that!

'Le progrès n'est point du tout une ligne droite à suivre; c'est une ligne en spirale qui a des courbes, des retours énormes sur elle-même, des interruptions si fortes qu'il ne recommence ensuite qu'avec peine et lentement.' (*Michelet.*)

Recent discoveries in Sir Thomas Bodley's Gallery show how the great and august were actually turned into decoration in the seventeenth century; how they were gathered together in an ornamental company, to preside not at the meals but at the labours of the learned. The use of this decorative sequence of portraits is worth remark, for the decoration of his Gallery was at least as important to Sir Thomas Bodley as the inspiration of their countenance. The Gallery with its carved and painted ceiling (disappeared) and its frieze of 200 portraits, must have pleased even Bodley himself, so stern about the admission of 'baggage-books' and other inferior matters into the building of his heart and labour. He had, of course, what is usually called 'a chance', since these, the already mighty dead, might be treated as the painter listed, and if he thought that Avicenna looked like that, who could cavil? The re-opening of this Gallery, the pride of the seventeenth-century devotee who created it, will be a fine addition to the portrait work of Oxford.

XXVIII

The Riding of the Cooks

1636. The bak'd meates served up in St. John's were so contrived by the cooks, that there was first ye formes of Archbishops, then Bishops, Doctors, etc., seene in order, wherein ye King and Courtiers tooke much content. Crosfield Diary
Therefore I will make haste away, onely asking this boone which will bee as good as a bone to the cookes, that your ladyship's servant Monsieur Piers may ride tomorrowe with the fierye fraternytie of his fellowe cookes and make upp the worthy companye of the round table which they are resolved not to leave till the whole house goe round with them.
Narcissus

THE Cook dwells so remote among the mighty and invisible movements of a College that it delights me to chronicle a snow-balling of cooks which I witnessed in an early hour of a Winter's morning outside the kitchen gate of Christ Church.

Having properly informed myself that I must on no account shoot bows and arrows in that precinct and resolved obediently not to do so, think of my astonishment in the silent delectable snow, to round the corner suddenly and come upon a group of figures from a picture of Peter Brueghel and the Middle Ages!

Under the high grey wall with its white pent-house roof of snow the frosty ammunition was flying well. The chefs' tall white hats, the kitchen boys' lesser white caps, the white linen coats all looked a fine Naples yellow against the dazzle of snow. But *how* the snowballs sped and thwacked! At the sound of a bell from within they all vanished with a whirl and nothing save the ruffled and scuffled snow at the gate told the story — until *I* do, as a prelude to my theme.

I have always enjoyed the learning and sententiousness of old cookery books. I like to know that the guests at my perfect dinner-party should number 'never fewer than the Graces but never more than the Muses'; that my soup should be 'as the prelude to the symphony'. I like to have my instructions from Sir Kenelm Digby to boil my eggs while I count 200 strokes of my pulse and to 'wait until my jelly simpers'; to know that my Lady Middlesex makes syllabubs for little glasses with spouts and to learn of Mrs. Raffald's 'nice whet for gentlemen'. To know that in 1440 the Coustarde Ryall was 'florisshed about with pomegranates and so served forth', and the tarte was 'couched in a coffin of paste and planted with pines' (kernels) — and to read of a 'subtlete' such as the Archbishops and Bishops and Doctors set out as dessert on the table of St. John's, pleases me as much as it pleased Charles I and Henrietta his queen. I should like also to have seen the 'Masterpieces' presented to the Guilds for status as Masters, when the Cooks had finished their time as journeymen, for though the

A College Cook

'subtletes' and set-pieces never in England, I think, reached the elaboration of those in the Italian Renaissance described by Vasari, in which artists and sculptors were employed, there still remain descriptions of them which show clearly enough the importance of a great man's or a College cook.

Cardinal Wolsey's Master-Cook wore 'every day', satin damask and velvet and 'wore a gold chain round his neck' — and his tour-de-force is impressive even to read about. 'Anon came up the second course with so many dishes, subtleties and curious devices *which were above an hundred in number* ... There were castles with images [statues] in the same; Paul's church and steeple in proportion for the quantity as well counter-feited as the painter should have painted it upon a cloth or wall. There were the beasts, birds, fowls of divers kinds and personages most lively made and counterfeit in dishes; some fighting as it were with swords, some with guns and cross-bows, some vaulting and leaping; some dancing with ladies, some in complete harness justing with spears ... among all, one I noted: there was a chess-board subtilely made of spiced plate with men to the same. ...'

No wonder Wolsey's Master-Cook wore a gold chain round his neck.

The College Chef has always been something of a figure in Oxford. Like the other 'Tradesmen' the cooks had a Guild of their own since 1453 with laws and customs of their own. (The cooks of the town had a separate guild and amalgamated with pastry-cooks and bakers.) They maintained a light in St. Mary's. They had a sermon preached to them in St. Peter in the East on Good Friday (no one on that day presumably requiring any dinner) and had a fine spectacular holiday called 'The Riding of the Cooks' on Whit Monday.

There are not many annals left of the Guild of Cooks. They were often men of substance. The Cook at Brasenose owned his own utensils and bequeathed them to the College. Another left his silver tankards to his College. Of the 'Cook's Buildings' at St. John's, 'The four chambers over the kitchen, together with the kitchen itself and cellar under it near to the west end of the Hall on the North side were built by Thomas Clarke the senior cook in 1613, the College then allowing him the rent of the said chambers for twenty years following'.

'The Rector and Fellows then ordered that the pension of forty shillings per annum issuing out of a tenement belonging to them in Magdalen parish of Oxford, (*which Luke Eaton their head-cook gave them*)' — should be given, etc.

Such men of substance seem to have been able to afford a handsome holiday, the expenses of which they bore themselves — not always amiably, I fear, for in 1463 there is an entry in the City Records of an appeal to the Commissary on the part of the two cooks appointed by the Gild to collect the money for their festival, against one of the Gild who will not contribute for the purpose of 'Coquorum annualis equitatio'. For so apparently serious a matter they appoint a day for investigation, and witnesses are produced in the absence of the defendant to prove the assertions of the Plaintiff.

Robert, Cook of Hampton Hall, 'deposeth that all the Cooks of the Colleges and

Halls have hitherto been accustomed to contribute to their annual feast; that he has been a cook for 6 years and that the cooks have always appointed two of their number to collect contributions'. Stephen, the cook of Vail Hall, corroborated the above testimony. 'Also Walter, another cook and John of Brasenose!'

The riding of the Cooks was, as one appreciates, a great occasion. And there one would leave it, as an amusing medieval junketing; the 'plump fraternytie of the cooks marching on their Governours' horses', riding down the Cowley Road to enter the East Gate, paying each one 4d. for a toll and so on through the High Street to the Feast. But an element of a kind enters in, mysterious and not explained, save by John Aubrey, who makes a sort of folk-lore solemnity about it. For the Cooks rode into the City to 'bring in the Fly', at Whitsun, and at Michaelmas rode out again to 'take out the Fly'. It was to the leper-church at Bartholomew's that they rode. This church (where there was a holy well frequented on May Day by the Fellows of Magdalen who sang songs to Flora and Spring and then walked home through groves and woods to a feast of their own) had become impoverished, and its hospital for lepers in a precarious condition, until the priest in charge, with the ingenuity of his kind, proclaimed an indulgence to those who visited the church and prayed at its altars, leaving a donation for the lepers. Thus the church became actually prosperous and the lepers lived in comfort, and it was this church which had the yearly patronage of the Gild of Oxford Cooks. Here they rode to fetch in the Fly — Gayton actually calls it 'the enemie the fly'.

It was an elaborately managed ceremony whose significance seems to have been lost. It seems to have no place in the end-of-Lent jollifications. The funeral of the sardine in Spain or the burial of the wooden herring in Poland at the church door on the last day of Lent were to mark the close of a period of fasting. But the Oxford cooks not only took out the Flie, but they had a special riding to *bring it in*. John Aubrey records: 'I remember at Oxford (before the Civill warres) the custom was that some day of ye Whitsun-holy dayes, of *de hoc* the Master-cooke (for that yeare) with the rest of his Brethren were marched in silke doublets on Horseback and rode, (I thinke) to Bartholemew's or Bullingdon Green to fetch in the Flye; the said master-cooke treated his brethren before they rode out (at Exeter College in 1642) I sawe them drinke their mornings draughts, and on Michaelmas day they rode thither again to carry the Fly away. Methinkes this old custome looks as if it were derived from that mentioned in Pliny.'

Pliny has indeed some entertaining uses for flies recorded, such as the habit of a Roman, thrice consul, who carried about with him a living fly wrapped in a piece of white linen to preserve him (which he vowed it did) from ophthalmia; but the nearest I could get to anything approaching the carrying out of the Flie was in a later passage.

'The Egyptians also invoke their Ibis against the incursions of serpents; and the people of Elis their god Myiagros and when the vast multitude of flies are bringing pestilence among them, the flies die immediately the propitiatory sacrifice has been made to this god.' Bk. x, chap. 40.

Another reference to the exodus of flies is in Bk. XXIX.

'It is generally believed that there is no creature less docile or intelligent than the fly; a circumstance which makes it all the more marvellous that at the sacred games at Olympia, immediately after the immolation of the god Myiodes, whole clouds of them take their departure from that territory.'

To which of these ceremonies, and why, John Aubrey refers, I cannot tell. Again, all these refer to the chasing away of flies, but not to bringing them in, and why the cooks should wish to bring his Ennemie *in* is puzzling. The manner of such speech seems to infer that there was an actual *object* which accompanied their riding — a banner perhaps or an emblem.

The custom seems obscure enough to be many centuries old and may have nothing to do with the obvious house fly after all if one becomes fanciful. The speech of Francis the Porter in the play *Narcissus* gives another origin for the ceremony. A young girl, deceived by a cook, filled the woods with her crying until the Dryads changed her to a butterfly and laid it as a symbol on the Cooks. So that it became a kind of joyful penance, unless, like the bringing in of the New Year and first-footing in Scotland, it was all symbolic and carried no emblem at all.

One can imagine the 'stout fraternitie of the cooks' jostling and pushing their way down the hill towards Oxford. Finery was allowed to the male in those days and if Master Wolsey's Cook was there with his gold chain leading the Master Cooks of other Colleges in silken doublets, it was an affair worthy to have been more fully chronicled. But the cook, like the actor, lives in the present. He has no immortality save that given him by others — there are few annals left of the University Cooks save an occasional record of their works. At one time these were so elaborate as to cause the University to set a limit to the amount to be spent on a banquet.

'In 1452 Neville, afterwards Archbishop of York, on his admission to the degree of Master of Arts, feasted the academics and many strangers for two successive days at two entertainments consisting of nine hundred costly dishes.' (*A. Wood.*)

1636. 'The excesse in ye feast found fault with and appointed a search in some olde bookes for a patterne in Dr. Airay's time, that more moderation be observed hereafter.'

Probably the old cookery-books were too thumbed to survive, but one would have liked to have seen those they used as a 'patterne'. I am perplexed to know how they helped the cooks or spenders on the feast to simplicity, for those of my acquaintance are terrifying in their prodigality.

'Take 1000 eggs or mo;' 'of whites of eggs take a great heape.' 'Let four men take the endes of the clothe and swing the cruddes.' The days of such magnificent eating are gone.

Turning over some archives in search of something else, I came on a curious entry which disclosed both the substantial and united standing of the University cooks. When the Elector Palatine, 'King of Bohemia', who left his name in a trail of public inns through the small towns of England, was defeated at White Mountain and fled to

England, his thrifty father-in-law James I made a collection for him which met with a generous response from all classes of the people, and important enough to be set down in the University accounts is 'Cooks' contribution to the King of Bohemia, Anno Domini 1620'.

XXIX

The Mistery of the Glovers

Marie Hamilton tae the kirk has gane
Wi' gloves upon her hands.

An English gentleman ought to wear six pairs of gloves a day. In the morning, to drive a
britzscha to the hunt, gloves of reindeer. At the hunt, to follow a fox, gloves of shammy leather.
To return to London in a Tilbury after a drive at Richmond in the morning, gloves of beaver.
To go later for a walk in Hyde Park, or to conduct a lady to pay her visits, coloured kid gloves,
braided. To go to a dinner party, yellow dog-skin gloves, and in the evening for a ball or a rout,
gloves of white lamb-skin embroidered with silk.

COUNT D'ORSAY (1801–52)

GLANCING carelessly at the newspaper for the country-side round Oxford,
one sees such and such an advertisement: 'Wanted, glove cutters for Worcester',
etc. 'Glove machinists wanted', etc., and spares little further thought to the
former importance of the guild and trade of glovers to the town and vicinity of Oxford.
Yet, 'at a wedding in 1604 the gloves given to the guests cost nearly £1,000'. (*Kyshe*.)
And the Court of Whitehall 1678 decreed that instead of a Bishop upon his consecration
presenting everyone who came to it with a pair of gloves, he was 'to pay £50 to the
rebuilding of the Catholic Church of St. Paul, which, as it is a pious work so will it
be some ease to the respective Bishops *in regard the expense of gloves did usually far exceed*
that sum'.

Some time ago a shop of repute in Oxford responded to the admonition of Press
and people to encourage home industries by arranging an exhibition of gloves from

109

local villages in their main windows. One was amazed at the number of villages which still produced first-class gloves; and the significance of the vicinity of many to the ancient deer-forests (Wychwood, Cornbury, Woodstock) did not escape one, nor how this craft has been kept alive from the days when 'a paire of gloves' from the city accounts was the proper gift to a visiting prince or noble, to the present day, when the only remaining ceremonial use of gloves is the presentation of a pair of white gloves to the Judge at a maiden assize.

The glove at first was purely a man's article of dress. Worn by a king, a judge, an ecclesiastic, it was a symbol of authority. Inferior people might not wear gloves in the presence of a bishop for instance. (I believe the only remaining link with this practice is the ceremony of presentation to the Pope where dress regulations forbid the wearing of gloves.)

There is an example of the ecclesiastical glove in the Ashmolean Museum where a pair of crimson silk gloves once used by William of Wykeham 1386 is exhibited. Another pair of white silk long-fingered gauntlets embroidered on the back with a rose is in the possession of New College. The figure in the portrait called William of Wykeham which hangs in the College wears a pair of white embroidered gloves of similar design.[1]

In the secular world there was first the heavy gauntlet for battle, and the glove for hawking. Then the glove for warmth took the place of the long sleeve; there were gloves of ceremony and authority, gloves of investiture and pardon. A king's glove on a pole was frequently the deputy for the presence of majesty to declare the legal opening of a Fair or Church, and the Law made great use of the glove of authority.

It is amusing to remember that when Defoe arranges the return of Robinson Crusoe to the island on which he has left the Spaniards, he puts among the necessities of civilization which he brings to them from home, so many pairs of gloves!

It was only after the Reformation that the glove became an article of female dress and then not so much so as to be included in Queen Elizabeth's sumptuary laws, and it was only when the glove became established as an article of dress, of women's dress in particular, that the guilds of glovers arose to protect their 'mistery' from the intrusion of 'foreigners' and of unauthorized workers.[2]

As early as 1463 Edward IV prohibited the importation of foreign gloves from abroad, but 'Foreigner' in its limited sense is used in the following petition by the Glovers of London:

1463. 'We have been informed that their families [the authentic London Glovers] are about 400 in number and upon them depending above 3,000 of our subjects who

---

[1] Let the curious visit the chapel of New College and there on the north side a misericord of the 14th century shows a Giant all ready for Jack at the top of his beanstalk, with a beautiful pair of gloves on his outstretched hands.

[2] In 1562 'The book of the mistery of glovers' was read before the Town Council and sealed with the town seal so that the same book be allowed by the justices of the Assize. *Records of the City of Oxford.*

A College Porter

are much decayed and impoverished by reason of the great confluence of persons of the same art, trade, or mystery, into our cities of London and Westminster from all parts of our Kingdom of England and Dominion of Wales, that for the most part have scarcely sewed any time thereto, working of gloves in chambers and corners, and taking apprentices under them, many in number, as well women as men, that become burdensome in the parishes wherein they inhabit and are a disordered multitude, living without proper government and making naughty and deceitful gloves.'

The art of the glover developed side by side with that of the important leather-maker (for leather was used for clothing, buckets and bottles and many other purposes) but was later in having a special Guild of its own. It was no light matter to belong to a Trade Guild. The term of apprenticeship for a glover was seven years. Every Guild assumed civic responsibilities. In 1625 'It is agreed that the Company of Glovers shall also be taxed towards the relief of the infected' (an epidemic in Oxford). As early as 1461 the Glovers were bound 'to find a light in All Hallows Church in the Trinity Chapel, namely 8 tapers and 6 torches to be honestly kept to the praise of the Holy Trinity'.

Whitsuntide was their festival and a mass was sung (later changed to prayers) on Trinity Monday in the Trinity Chapel of All Saint's Church before the election of officers. It was supposed that the heavy taxation of the Guild members led to a settling of the trade in the villages outside the five mile radius beyond which no one might belong to any City Guild. But it was probably also the easy access to their material and in the days of hand stitching the possibility of distributing the work among women and girls in their own houses and the cheapness of work done in the country. Deer-skin and sheep-skin gloves for hunting and hawking were made in the neighbourhood of the forests, Woodstock having its special fame.

Of the glove industry at this place, which became important especially when Blenheim Palace was built, and of its development to the present, there is an engrossing paper (*Oxoniensia*, Vol. III, 1938) by Miss T. E. Schulz. But entry after entry in the Civic Records show how important the manufacture of gloves was to the City of Oxford.

1628. 'They may not spend out of the common stock except it bee for the necessary use and credit of the Cyttie, as in giving gloves to Noblemen when they come to the Cyttie.' 1619. 'In place of customary gifts of "new ashen bowles and dishes" by new bailliffs to the Mayor, there was the following order.

'And the scope and meaning of this House being now to do a particular good to Citizens before strangers, as well for that consideration as for more ornament and decorum in the Kynd of gift, not take away the gift or the custom thereof, but only to change it into a more acceptable gift, doe hereby enact and order that forever hereinafter, in lieu of those bowles and dishes, gloves shall be given of all these rates to all that are of this House. viz.
To Mr. Mayor of the time being a paire of 2/6
To every Alderman a paire of 2/-

To every of the rest of the thirteene a paire of 18d.

To the Bailliffs for the yeare a paire of 18d. a piece.

To the the two Chamberlaynes for the yeare each man a paire of 12d.

To everyone of the house that hath been Bailey or hath a Bailey's place a paire of 12d.

To every Chamberlayne or that hath a Chamberlayne's place a paire of 10d.

To everyone of the Common Counsell a paire of 8d. and all and every the same gloves from tyme to tyme to be bought *of some freeman resident and abydying in Oxford or the suburbs thereof, which is a glover of this cittie and of no other glover whatsoever.*'

The expenses occurred in the giving of gloves to visitors was more frequent both in College and City accounts than the entries for sanitation. Henrietta Maria was given a pair of gloves costing £30. James I was presented with 'two pairs of Oxford gloves with a deep fringe of gold, the turnovers being wrought with pearl' (1605).

A pair of Queen Elizabeth's gloves are in the Ashmolean Museum. Her gloves were frequently perfumed[1] and in the year 1631 an entry is made in the accounts of Trinity College 'pro fumigandis chirothecis'.

The pretty wife of Samuel Pepys was indulged by him very sweetly in this new mode.

'He hath also brought a great many gloves perfumed, of several sorts, but all too big by half for her, and yet she will have two or three dozens of them.'

'I did give each of them a pair of Jesimy plain gloves and another of white.'

'Gloves given away £10. 4. 6.' seems quite a prosaic expenditure for the city fathers. 'The citty's gift of gloves' was given to Queen Anne in 1702.

Occasionally there is a touch of personality in the entry. 'For bestowing a paire of gloves upon our Visitor the Archbishop of Yorke 30/- price or thereabouts in ye name of ye College, *though we have no occasion to use him.*'

For performing some service for Brasenose College in 1657, Brokesby, the schoolmaster of Birmingham, 'received two paires of gloves with black fingers and a paire of white kid leather gloves'.

'Here I met Sir. G. Downing, who would speak with me, and first to enquire what I paid for my kid leather gloves I had on my hand, and shewed me others of his, as handsome, as good in all points, cost him but 12d. a pair, and mine me 2s. He told me he had been seven years finding out a man that could dress English sheep-skin as it

---

[1] Jessimin the flowers of which are of a delicate sweet smell and often used to perfume gloves. Edmund Howes, Stow's continuator, informs us that sweet or perfumed gloves were first brought into England by the E. of Oxford on his return from Italy, in the 15th year of Queen Elizabeth, during whose reign and long afterwards they were very fashionable. They are frequently mentioned by Shakespeare. Autolycus in the Winter's Tale has among his wares

'Gloves as sweet as damask roses.'

A Footnote to Pepys's Diary

Even the greatest minds were not displeased to dally with the idea. In W. D. Caröe, *Wren and Tom Tower*, there occurs this passage: 'It is somewhat curious to observe Wren's versatility . . . He presided at a meeting of the Council and a General Meeting [of the Royal Society] on March 23rd, 1681, when he discoursed upon the perfuming of gloves with Pessamine.'

should be — and indeed, it is now as good, in all respects, as kid, and he says will save £100,000 a year, that goes out to France for kid skins.' (*Pepys.*)

'For a glove to be good, three realms must have contributed to it. Spain to prepare the skin; France to cut it, and England to sew it.' But it was France which finally captured the imagination of the luxurious by her production of the fine kid glove. In spite of prohibition the delicate things claimed priority. Though Limerick for a time made a glove 'so fine that it could be enclosed in a walnut shell', it was the heavy type of glove which England and Oxford were left to produce. York and Hexham tans and sheep skins, Hereford beavers, Yeovil military gloves; Ludlow, Leominster, Worcester, Oxford, etc., all made and were unsurpassed in making the strong wearing glove of England. There is, nevertheless, the suggestion of imported goods when John Verney in 1680 sends a paper box to Sir Ralph, containing 'In a paper sealed a Paire of white gloves and a paire of coloured gloves laced with black Flanders lace; and if ye fingers bee too long for you, Thom. Hobart sayeth hee will alter them for you when in towne. All Genoa gloves are long-fingered. A paire of greene fingered gloves for my Brother. White and coloured lace gloves for my sister. Pink Couloured trimd gloves for Master Ralph, Skye Coloured trimd gloves for Master Munsey. White gloves trimmed with green etc. for my little niece'. There are still glovers who remember the piece-making of gloves round the villages of Woodstock and its neighbourhood. Mr. Fardon the glover has written of his boyhood and the changes which have come about to the glovers as to other mysteries. In spite of decline in the 'mistery of the glovers' it is still a pleasant experience to buy one's gloves at Woodstock.

At a recent visit to the Pullman Grove Factory there, I was shown how the ancient craft is substantially unchanged. All gloves are still cut by hand; the skins are stretched and worked without machinery and the stitching of gloves is still carried on in the cottages, though the distributing agent is now not a pony but a motor-car.

XXX

'Belt-Makers, Deformers, Shavers of Nature'

The crispèd brooks
With mazy error under pendant shades
Ran nectar, visiting each plant, and fed
Flowers worthy of Paradise, which not nice art
In beds and curious knots, but nature boon
Pour'd forth profuse on hill and dale and plain
Both where the morning sun first warmly smote
The open field and where the unpierced shade
Inbrowned the noontide bowers. Thus was the place
A happy rural seat of various view.

MILTON

In the garden of the Marshal de Biron at Paris, consisting of 14 acres, every walk is buttoned on
each side by lines of flowerpots, which succeed in their season. When I saw it there were 9000
pots of asters La Reine Marguerite.

HORACE WALPOLE

WHEN Horace Walpole, that elegant advocate of the modern garden, discovered that the ideal landscape-garden had indeed been ideally planned
and described by a blind poet, he chronicled also his surprise that a century
had passed before anyone was quick-witted enough to put practical shape to Milton's
imaginary Eden. Satire indeed (not only Mr. Walpole's) was active in its attack on the
English formal garden in its decline.

'At Lady Oxford's at Piddleton in Dorsetshire, there was when my brother married,
a double enclosure of thirteen gardens, each, I suppose, not more than a hundred yards
square, with an enfilade of correspondent gates, and before you arrived at these, you
passed a narrow gut between two stone terraces that rose above your head and which
was crowned by a line of pyramidal yews. A bowling green was all the lawn admitted
in those times; a circular lake the extent of magnificence.'

'Parterres embroidered in flowers like a petticoat.' (I believe Francis Bacon called
them jam-tarts.) 'Waterworks to wet the unwary.' 'Walls built to exclude the view and
then mounds built inside to climb up and look over at it.' 'Stairs for going up and down
in the open air, (his pet abomination)' and the crowning absurdity of the 'arbour',
which he interpreted as 'setting aside a portion of your garden to be melancholy in', all
these conceits, running in the eighteenth century to extravagance, roused Mr. Walpole's
derision. His friend, and neighbour Pope joined him both in satire and in making
a garden at Twickenham after the new manner of Kent and Repton and Capability

114

Encaenia Garden Party

Brown, who broke down walls, invented the Fosse and the Ha Ha, thus joining a landscape view to the immediate privacy of the house.

Shenstone the poet spent a fortune on his landscape garden.

'Now was excited his delight in rural pleasures and his ambition of rural elegance, to entangle his walks and to wind his waters; which he did with such judgement and such fancy as made his little domain the envy of the great and the admiration of the skilful; a place to be visited by travellers and copied by designers. Whether to plant a walk in undulating curves and to place a bend at every turn where there is an object to catch the view; to make water run where it will be heard and to stagnate where it will be seen; to leave intervals where the eye will be pleased and to thicken the plantation where there is something to be hidden, demands any great powers of mind I will not inquire. Perhaps a sullen and surly spectator may think such performances rather the sport than the business of human reason. But it must be at least confessed, that to embellish the form of nature is an innocent amusement and some praise must be allowed by the most supercilious observer to him who does best what such multitudes are content to do well.' (*Johnson.*)

Dr. Johnson then, it seems, gave a measured approval to the new movement. Walter Scott's hero was more guarded. 'I would not deface a scene of natural grandeur or beauty by the introduction of crowded artificial decorations; yet such may, I think, be very interesting where the situation, in its natural state, otherwise has no particular charms. So that, when I have a country house — who can say how soon? — you may look for grottoes and cascades and fountains; nay, if you vex me by contradiction perhaps I may go the length of a temple!'

Southey was among those who wished tradition to be prolonged. Of Trinity garden he wrote: 'The garden here is remarkable for a wall of yew which encloses it on three sides, cut into regular pilasters and compartments ... I should lament if a thing which is so perfect of its kind and which has been raised with so many years of care — indeed with so many generations — were to be destroyed because it does not suit with the modern improved taste in gardening.'

The index to John Evelyn's *Elysium Britannicum* contains such a bewildering list of the necessities of the vanishing formal garden

'Of Knots, Parterres, Compartments, Borders and Embossments.
Of Walks, Terraces, Carpets and Alleys, Bowling-greens, Malls.
Of Groves, Labyrinths, Daedales, Cabinets, Cradles, Pavilions,
Galleries, Close, Walks and other Relievos.
Of Fountains, Cascades, Runlets, Piscinas and Waterworks.
Of Rocks, Grots, Cryptes, Mounts, Precipices, Porticos, Venteducts.
Of Statues, Columns, Dials, Perspectives, Pots, Vases.
Of artificial echoes, music and Hydraulic motion'

that the word *formidable* seems more apt for such a garden than *formal* — yet these mechanics were wholly admired in their day. John Evelyn speaks with an appreciation which would exasperate Horace Walpole about some 'agreeable cheats' he discovered on a visit to one famous garden. Two musketeers cut in yew discharged jets of water upon the unwary person who opened an adjoining gate. These 'pleasant deceits' as he calls them in another place would hardly commend themselves to the present sense of humour.

The Diary of Thomas Blaikie, a Scots gardener who was employed by Marie Antoinette and other French patricians to reform the old gardens and remodel them as 'English Gardens' shows how enthusiastically the fashion spread in France. He describes what he was called upon to destroy. In the garden of Monceau: 'There were monuments of all sorts, Countrys and Ages, but placed in such a manner that from every part there was a confused landskipe, for there was adjoining Chinese and Gothick buildings, Egyptian Pyramides joined to Italian vineyards. The whole was a small confusion of many things joined together without any great natural plan.' 'The small confusion of many things joined together,' was what the Lansdcape gardeners set out to hunt from the gardens. But, in reading Thomas Blaikie, I confess to a little private nostalgia at this point. How I should have loved to see, in my *'Oxford which was never built',* just one corner left in a garden for a 'Chambre des Philosophes', or a 'Tombeau de Mahomet'.

But Milton planned an Eden and Mr. Walpole was concerned with the seats of noblemen where the landscape garden was first and most suitably designed, and the names of the by-gone fancies of formal gardeners were very charming — the pleached alley and camomile lawn; the banks of wild thyme for resting, the Grove for Shade and quiet. The pleached alley remains at Trinity, The Grove at Magdalen and Merton, and the mound in New College. Blenheim still has the Knot, and the water-garden — the water-garden which was introduced into England from Italy by those who remembered the beauty of tinkling water in the heavy Italian heat and forgot the rain of an English heaven.

But the garden as we know it in Oxford began long ago and was fostered by a strange old gardener called Jacob Bobart who was set to look after the physick garden for the University.

'After the walks and gates of this famous garden were built old Jacob Bobart (1632) may be said to be ye man yt first gave life and beauty to this famous place, who by his care and industry replenished the walls with all manner of good fruits our climate would ripen and bedeck the earth with great variety of trees, plants and exotick flowers, dayly augmented by the Botanists who bring them hither from ye remote Quarters of ye New World.'

The formal garden and topiary work were much favoured by this cheerful old man, who, besides trimming the trees, had the engaging habit of hanging silver tags on to his beard on all holiday occasions. In an early Oxford Almanack, Jacob Bobart the elder represents one of the 'avocations' of the University, and is drawn with a pruning-hook almost as big as himself. Poems were written to the clipped yews which he planted on either side of the North Gate 'that one being the first built': (Poor Anthony Wood!) 'Grown up to be gigantick bulkey fellows, one holding a Bill, th'other a club on his shoulder.' Both were about 30ft high. Prettier still I should think were 'two pilasters of the same work each with a vase of flowers artistically cut and very pretty'.

I once took a Swedish lady round some College gardens. Her agitation mounting with her admiration she at last burst out, 'It is too good for boys! It is far too good for boys!' That is how some people see it!

Just at what point the garden became a serious part of Oxford College amenities it would be difficult to say. It began in the monastic cloister and graveyard one thinks, and developed after each century's special pattern. 'This College, (Magdalen) was brought to such perfection, that nothing has been added to it in my time, and in some respects it doth exceed all other colleges, for most of ye Fellowes have convenient gardens and private stables, each man apart for his own horse. These other adjuncts of beauty and convenience hereto, belonging, is their Bowling-green, delicate walks of their own of great length by the Cherwell, and when they please to stir a little, in those of ye Physick Garden and up the hill towards Headington.'

Interference with existing conditions was not always kindly received. Hearne has a deplorable story to tell of Dr. Hudson of University College who tried, on his appointment as Bursar, to 'regulate divers disorders relating to his office'.

'Among these laudable undertakings is chiefly to be mentioned the College Garden, which having been almost ruinated and quite out of repair, he ordered to be covered with Green Turff, planted with Trees and flowers and the Walks to be gravelled, to ye great Beauty of ye Place and satisfaction of the rest of ye Fellows; and there was no one of ye College appeared at present displeased with it but ye Master (a commoner of ye House and Nephew to Mr. Smith lately Senior Fellow and now in London who it seems was always averse to this Reform) a day or two after it was finished, with two or three more of ye College, got into ye Garden in ye Night time, pull'd up some of ye Ews, spoil'd others and did other mischief, to ye no small grief of ye Doctor and ye rest of ye Fellows, it being such a piece of malice as one would think could not enter into the thoughts of any person of common Breeding and indeed seldom or never heard of in ye University but in ys College where they have had some other instances of ye same Nature and have had some lads noted for this Diabolical wickedness.'

Looking over old prints of College gardens what astonishes one is the immense confidence required by the new gardeners. The wholesale destruction of those high clipped yew walls; the cost and labour of reconstructing the gardens, needed at least the complaisance of 'Capability Brown' (so called because he invariably saw 'capabilities' in a scheme) who, having used some minor Thames water to raise the level of his lake at Blenheim exclaimed, 'Thames! Thames! you will never forgive me', for such projects, and shows the spirit of the dauntless new-mode gardeners. From them we gained a nation-wide love of flowers, of forest and flowering trees and of wide and sunny lawns, for fashion and progress overwhelmed the protests, and the great yew enclosures and topiary curiosities were felled. They were not all in the best condition. Von Offenbach says of the Physick Garden that 'the rarer plants are all at the end of the garden locked up; the middle of the garden as already mentioned above, has a wild appearance, with all sorts of common vegetables.' And what an addiction to 'bowers' the old College gardeners had — 'An Oxonian garden, of the period under consideration, was never thought in a condition that would endure critical inspection until it was furnished with at least one arbour of living shrubbery', says Jeaffreson, and goes on by the help of Loggan prints to disclose these 'grots'. Balliol had three arbours; Oriel a 'bower'; University 'an enormous arbour', New College an arbour on a bowling-green, Pembroke was 'lavishly provided with bowers', etc. It was evident that 'setting aside a portion of your garden to be melancholy in' had grown beyond a habit into a conviction. Judging from the old prints most of the College gardens were no more than alleys or plots and their planting no more interesting than the setting of trimmed green trees on a flat ground, like the triangular trees on wooden stands which used to come in boxes of bricks for children long ago from Germany.

It is in St. John's garden that one would have held one's breath as the high yew walls crashed down; for there were two rectangular gardens enclosed by yews, clipped into the shape of walls at a man's height from the ground, the trunks forming a colonnade like the arcade of a cloister. They probably served little other purpose than that of keeping out the sun, and, in the light of later developments such formidable alleys were best uprooted, but it must have required courage to begin! It was evident that the formal gardens had their drawbacks and that travellers said so. We need to go no farther than the journey-book of Zacharias Conrad Von Offenbach (1710) to be electrically aware of this. He, a German, setting out with the guide-book of a Frenchman (*Délices d'Angleterre*) to visit England, was heading for disillusion; but he was, if acidulated, at least candid, and to be candid upon past affairs creates a pleasant attitude of attention in the reader of the present. He thought the Oxford gardens lacking in air. 'Merton garden consists of a shrubbery and some low dark shrubs which are not really pleasant as they have no fresh air.' New College was 'a very mediocre garden consisting of three walls and four flower beds' — In Trinity are 'neither trees or shrubs, nothing but grass plots and some small yews'. Most of the gardens were almost usurped by topiary work carried to extravagant lengths — New College had a sundial of trimmed box with a peat stake supplying the finger. It was all better done in Germany and the 'Délices d'Angleterre' were still (for Count Von Offenbach) to seek.

Topiary work and grass plots may have had a practical reason for their ubiquity, for the clipping of shaped trees takes place at only one time of the year and the grass plot lies dormant in winter. But the new gardeners had their way. The modelled trees and yew hedges crashed. The wind of variety was awake and ruffled its passages straight through the Oxford gardens.

Something distressing seems to have happened to the Bobart family during its

Magdalen Tower from Botanic Gardens

ascent in three generations — from gardener (Jacob Bobart) to Professor of Botany (William), for the candid friend of Oxford, Von Offenbach, writes, 'I was greatly shocked by the hideous features and generally villainous appearance of this good and honest man. His wife, a filthy old hag, was with him, and although she may be the ugliest of her sex, he is certainly the most repulsive of the two'. And old Jacob had been such a figure too, with his beard of silver tassels! Perhaps Von Offenbach had just been shocked by the discovery that learned Oxford called a College *Corpus* Christi instead of *Corporis* Christi as he is sure it should be. Perhaps even, disliking English food as much as the 'anticks' in the cloister at Magdalen (which he allowed might be excused if Dr. Sacheverell were stuck up among them) he had even on that particular day 'dined with Duke Humphrey'. He was certainly not amused.

Mr. Jeaffreson attributes the improvement in the College gardens to the gradual infiltration of women; the marriages of the Heads of the Houses and the taking over, (not without protest) of the lady in office, of the private gardens, and points out that even if the eighteenth century swept away the formal garden, this old-fashioned arrangement was at any rate a great deal better than that existing before Elizabeth's time. Some of the credit for the later interest taken in the gardens, for the sake of flowers and their beauty and the ornamental disposal of flowers must, I think, be given to old Jacob of the Physick garden, who attracted visitors to this earliest attempt at a Botanical garden and aroused interest in the flowers and trees for their own sake.

'They shouldn't give all that to boys!' said a Canadian officer to me, echoing the protest of the earlier Swedish lady. But the 'boys' gave a great deal of it *themselves*, one must remember, which is one of the happiest facts to recall in every aspect of Oxford life.

The decline of the landscape garden came with imitation and the attempt to apply to small urban plots designs more suitable for Hampton Court. It was not in the great estates, but in the small town-gardens, that the landscape gardeners made their mistakes, and the 'belt-makers' had their head. The funereal shrubberies of the suburbs darkened for half a century the gardens of Victoria and Edward, and Satire stung now, not the formalists but the free gardeners.

> 'Prim gravel walks through which we winding go
> In endless serpentines that nothing shew
> Till tired I ask, why this eternal round?
> And the pert gardener says, " 'Tis pleasure-ground"!'

Some of the College gardens reflect even yet their old likeness. The water-walks of Magdalen are much as they always were; the terrace-walks in the Fellows' garden at Merton (though higher than its original building intention) with the tiny pavilion and the elegant ironwork and the avenue of limes convey still a good deal of dignity and spaciousness of gardening which carried the architecture of noble building just a little further out of doors. The December sun sends a transitory and mournful gleam across the sward. Frost has stung the berries of the cotoneaster on the grey wall to a sharper scarlet. The gardeners have gone home. Only a quiet old fire of leaves smoulders on alone under the trees. To every garden in whatever century there return the kindly occupations of gardening.

OLD SHELDONIAN TERMINAL
CORPUS GARDEN

XXXI

'The Expressive Stain'

And sooth to seyn, my chamber was
Full well depainted, and with glass
Were all the windows well y-glazed
Full clean and nat an hole y-crazed,
That to behold it was great joy
For wholly all the story of Troy
Was in the glazing y-wrought thus,
Of Hector and King Priamus,
Of Achillis and of Laomedon
And eke of Medea and of Jason
Of Paris, Helen and of Levine.   CHAUCER

WHAT is that very strange window in the North aisle of the cathedral?' asked a lady of me. 'You must know it, I think. There is a man sitting under a tree with a town behind.'

'The Jonah window,' I suggested.

'Oh, Jonah! Probably it is! Such a strange window,' she added pensively retrospective.

One remembered all at once the pleasure one had had from the old painted landscape windows in the country churches of Holland, where whole Biblical stories live between you and the sky and create the glory of those roomy and stately old Protestant churches; such a type of landscape window, which, in the cathedral of Christ Church, had aroused the lady's interest.

Though Anthony Wood called the painter of the Jonah Window a 'Dutchman',

121

it was from Emden that Abram Van Linge came with his brother Bernard, also a glass-painter, and since both glass-workers did a good deal of work in Oxford Colleges it is worth while lingering on that accomplished by the younger of the two brothers — Abram.

They are not of the great period of stained-glass workers. Indeed, there are purists who maintain that their methods illustrate a definite and final decline in the technique of glass-staining. There are those who think also, that the subjects attempted are beyond the limits of the medium. That spurious methods were used to carry out unsuitable ambitions. That colour deteriorated in the new (and not very durable) processes of enamel painting, and that the conventions of stained glass are not those of picture-painting. But of those workers in the foreign and fashionable methods of glass-painting in the seventeenth century the Van Linges were among the best who worked in England.

The making of coloured glass is a simple enough story. In the beginning, glass of any kind, whether plain or coloured, could only be made in small pieces, and the substance, if coloured, was dyed throughout, the colour being incorporated in the molten glass. Given these small pieces of coloured glass, the window-builder set to work to arrange them against the light in his pattern, like a mosaic, the pieces of coloured glass being held in place by their leaden lines. In such a method what mattered even more than design was the translucency and brilliance of the colours, reproducing, as they seemed at first intended to do, the vivid and jewel-like enamels of the East from which the first stained-glass workers seemed to have derived their impulse.[1] This method, from the very limitation of the material and colours, produced a highly formal and stylized form of Art, the work as much of the craftsman as the artist. Fourteen late-thirteenth-century windows in the choir of Merton College Chapel and four in St. Michael's Church belong to this early period. They are the oldest in Oxford.

But with the discovery of the vaulted roof and the wide window-spaces which displaced the barrel-vaulted roof and low sturdy pillar of the Norman builders, the window became more important. Instead of wide spaces of wall to be covered with painting, there were the transparencies of windows, supported by tracery, to be filled. The possibility of decorating these began to attract more ambitious artists and the fourteenth century onwards brought the magnificent stained windows of which so many still remain. At times the width of the window spaces was to be in itself a snare, as in the Sainte Chapelle in Paris where you cannot see the windows for the glass.

The small pieces of pot-metal glass with which the early windows had been filled were now inadequate, and chemistry was awaking to other discoveries. The two important developments of the fourteenth and early fifteenth centuries were *flashed glass* and *silver-stain*. Before the discovery of flashed glass very little was done in the way of

[1] There is a curious instance of the affinity between coloured glass and enamel mentioned by Professor Lethaby; a silver wine-cup (*c.*1320) in which small windows with tracery complete and filled with transparent enamel are let in to the sides of the wine-cup to illuminate the heart of the wine.

The Broad from Trinity Gates

shading or drawing. Rudimentary outlining by painting on top of pot-metal glass was the utmost attempted. But flashed glass (described also as 'coated glass'), one layer of colour on top of another or on top of white glass, made by blowing a bubble of white glass and then dipping it into molten colour, cutting open and flattening so making two layers of different tints, gave further possibilities for experiment. Heavy colours like ruby, which in the early pot-metal glass were barely transparent, could be lightened in tone by the white underlay, and the new technique of abrading the coloured surface by scraping it with special tools to required degrees of light and dark, opened out a more varied pictorial treatment. The discovery of silver-stain, a process by which certain silver-deposits dropped into the molten glass produced a vivid gold stain, added greatly to the beauty and liveliness of the fifteenth-century glass. This discovery flooded the windows with golden glories — haloes, hair of saints, crowns, thrones, borders of kingly robes — the glass of that century shows them everywhere. The windows of the Library of Trinity College have this sunny quality and so has the head of the Virgin in the Lucy Chapel, Christ Church, a bare outline whose beauty is in its over-shadowing gold.

The period of the Jonah window was in one sense a revival of the interest in window-painting, but a period which marks the decline of the classic method of filling a light with coloured glass supported with lead lines. The glass-workers began to develop other methods and in the case of Abram Van Linge who signs his name on the window in the cathedral, the space of the window is treated as a painter treats his canvas, as an empty space to be covered with a painted design. New chemical methods were again tried. The Van Linges, both Bernard and Abram, used an enamelling process, first to heighten tones already in the pot-metal glass, and then as the sole medium for their purposes.

'Enamel painting is simply painting on sheets of white glass with prepared colours in the same way as one paints in oil or water colours. Each colour — local colour, shadows and outline, is applied with the brush, a great contrast to pot-metal work in which the local colour is supplied by the glass itself. When the picture or design is finished, the sheet is placed in the Kiln and the work is completed in the same way as a pot-metal window.' (F. S. Eden.)

In 674 Wilfred, Archbishop of York, filled the windows of the cathedral, then open to the weather, with glass, 'such glass', says Edius, 'as permitted the sun to shine therein'. Benedict Biscop, the wealthy ecclesiastical collector, having been on a journey to Rome with Wilfred, and having a great church at Jarrow in building, also sent for workmen and glaziers from France (the centre of the glass industry) to fill his windows with coloured glass 'after the Roman manner'. As the building of great cathedrals progressed, it became the practice of the pious to set handsome windows within them as memorial offerings. This practice of glazing a window as an act of insurance to Heaven — the figure and name of the donor often being as important as that of the saint — was severely trounced by Langland in his *Vision of Piers the Plowman*.

'And sithen he seyde.
We have a windowe a-wirchyng, will sitten us ful heigh. [Cost us a great deal.]
Woldestow glase that gable and grave there-in thy name.
Siker sholde thy soule be, hevenne to have.'

But since the wish to enrich a church with a beautiful object need not be the prompting of an inferior nature, the practice continued, and others besides Bishop Benedict sent for workmen from abroad to glaze windows in England. In the case of the Van Linges it was Laud who, if he didn't actually *send* for, at least encouraged them when they came; whether by advice of Nicholas Stone who had his training in Flanders, and must have known, at least by repute, all the craftmen of his time there, I am unable to state, but believe it to be at least probable. Dutchmen had been sent before to glaze windows in England. Glass-painters from Flanders had been employed both by Henry VII and Henry VIII and they brought their methods with them to this country, which, it may be remembered, produced no coloured glass until very late. So that the English glaziers were entirely dependent upon Continental workshops for their materials. In 1447 for instance 'John Prudde of Westminster glazier — covenanteth to glaze all the windows in the new chapell in Warwick *with glasse beyond the sea* and *with no glasse of England,* and that in the finest ware, with the best, cleanest, and strongest *glasse of beyond the seas* that can be had in England' — So that if the supply of 'glasse beyond the sea' was in any way interrupted — either by 'Act of God' as in the Black Death abroad which caused English workman to refuse to unload glass from foreign ships lest the plague come with it, or by any devilry of man such as the persecution, dispersal and final extermination of the Huguenot glass-makers in the Province of Lorraine, as a consequence of which supplies of glass came to almost a standstill — new methods and experiments were inevitably tried, or the glass-workers harked back to experiments and discoveries of former years which had been attempted perhaps but not carried to conclusion. Waves of method advanced and receded and now and then one wave would advance the tide and Abram Van Linge 'worked at a point where painting had overtaken the mosaic work and overwhelmed it'. The shortage of coloured glass from abroad may easily have forced the method he finally adopted and developed, but adventure was in the air. It is easy to see how, given a brush to experiment with, and much more variety of colour than could be obtained in the pot-metal glass, having also in mind the noble schools of painting of his own day, a picture with landscape and perspective (all wrong from the orthodox standard) seemed a more advanced form of art for the filling of a window-space than the earlier mosaic type of window, which in any case, since the shortage of glass from abroad, became difficult to compass. And the new method, used by the Van Linges with cleverness and success, was conquering the glass-workers' shops.

The cosmopolitan aspect of the art of that century, with its face turned towards the great serene painting of Italy is strongly reflected in the art of the Netherlands, and some of its happiest conventions can be recognized in the painting of the Jonah window; from the intimate figure and literal yellow gourds of the foreground, to the perspective of the landscape reaching onward to high and ineffable blue mountains, and carrying the city of Nineveh up to heaven. The Low Countries have few hilly districts and I cannot recall any 'city set on a hill'. But Italy abounds in little hill towns and nebulous mountains, and it is these memories which flicker and glance in Abram Van Linge's window. Such a picture, such a landscape, could be more easily produced by a brush and variegated colours, and the Van Linges adopted the method of enamel-painting. The practice must have pleased their contemporaries for there is a substantial amount of their work still left even in Oxford whence much glass has vanished.

Where did all the glass go to which has disappeared from the chapels and halls of the University? An easy way out is to say that the Reformers broke it, but it is not so simple a tale as that. True, Queen Elizabeth ordered white glass to be put into the churches, but then, so did the Cistercian Order long before the Reformation, and a good deal of coloured glass was actually left in because of the expense of refilling the windows with other material. The bulky shoulders of Cromwell have been burdened with blame, yet the Protector can hardly have been responsible for the taking down of eight coloured windows from the Cathedral of Chartres and the substitution of white glass in the tracery, and it was Fairfax the Puritan who protected the glass of York Minster. Anthony Wood was interested in the glass of the University and has tabled what was in existence in his day. His comments throw a faint light upon its fate.

'And besides all this, *that they might add more light,* took away the old painted glass in the east window and much of the crustation and arched work as well as that of other windows in the chapel.' (St. John's.) The rebuilding or alterations of Colleges and Chapels led to careless usage of glass and much disappeared in this way; for not all glass was of a sacred or emblematic character nor was it even in the churches. Portraits of benefactors, founders and great men of the Colleges would be worked in glass in windows of libraries and halls. Coats of arms, rebuses and verses filled the windows and quite as much of this secular glass has gone as that from the churches. Wood mentions the story of King Alfred 'very lively in glass' in University College, a college which seems to have been unusually rich in painted glass, for he writes: 'In most of the chamber windows of the little old quadrangle which was *pulled down to make room for this that was so uniform,* were divers inscriptions, arms and rebuses, put up in memory of the benefactors thereunto, but most of them having long before my time quite broken or taken away, I could never (though much I have endeavoured) achieve more than what follows'. Elsewhere he speaks of a window in which were 'certain pictures that were broken, confused or misplaced'.

Mr. F. S. Eden believes that large quantities of coloured glass from the dispossessed religious houses were traded on the continent. He quoted a contemporary French glass painter, Bernard Torlissy, who says, that 'in the later years of the sixteenth century, painted glass was so little esteemed in France that it was handed about the country by dealers in old clothes and such like refuse'. But the disposal of painted glass by sale was not confined to dispossessed convents. Such a structural alteration to University College as that mentioned above when a whole quadrangle was rebuilt and the glass no longer fitted the new windows, led to a wholesale disposal of old glass, and there were actual 'deals' proposed even in high places. Aubrey mentions the offer of Gondomar the Spanish Ambassador in the reign of James I, who openly 'offered a goode summe for windowes of great value' in Edmund Rich's church of Salisbury, and the much quoted letter of John Bury 1788 discloses another channel of disappearance;

Sir: this day I have sent you a box full of old stained and painted glass, as you have desired me to due, which I hope will sute your Purpos, it is the best I can get at Present. But I expect to beate too Peaces a great deal very sune, as it is of no use to me and wee do it for the lead. If you want any more of the same sortes you may have what thear is, if it will pay for taking out as it is a Deal of Trouble to what Beating it to Peaces his; you will send me a line soon as Possoble, for we are goain to move our glasing shop to a Nother plase, and then we hope to save [*sic*] a great deal more of the like sort, which I ham your most humble servant.   JOHN BURY

Ancient glass gives place to modern as changes of taste occur. New College disposed of an old window to fill the tracery with Sir Joshua Reynolds's design. That this was in the mode of the century is attested by Warton's lines on the change.

> 'Lo, from the canvas, Beauty shifts his throne,
> Lo, Picture's powers a new formation own;
> Behold, she prints upon the crystal plain
> With her own energy, th'expressive stain;
> The mighty master spreads his mimic toil
> More wide, nor only blends the breathing oil;
> But calls the lineaments of life complete
> From genial alchemy's creative heat
> Obedient forms to the bright fusion gives
> While in the warm enamel nature lives.'

But in the words of museum catalogues 'This work is not now esteemed'.

Now and again people have been tried in courts for taking the law into their own hands and breaking glass which they thought offensive. The little Recorder of Salisbury, Henry Sherfield (1632), who was brought before the Star Chamber for breaking some windows in his own town, had a spirited defence. 'He saith that this window and the painting thereon was not a true representation of the Creation, for that it contained divers forms of little old men in blue and red coats, and naked in the hands and feet for the picture of God the Father . . . The defendant conceiveth this to be false, for there is but one God and this representeth seven Gods etc.'

Economy too played its part in the disappearance of glass from windows, for Aubrey tells how William Camden came to see the church at Yatton Keynell and 'particularly took notice of a little painted glasse windowe in the chancell which (ever since my remembrance) haz been walled up to save the parson the chardge of glasing it'. Stained glass was retained in churches for a similar reason, because it was too expensive to replace it with new white glass. But it is evident there was a great deal of painted glass in Oxford. John Aubrey confirms that every county had several glass workers.

'When I came to Oxford, crucifixes were common in the glasse windowes, in the studies windowes and in the chamber windowes were canonized saints (e.g. in my chamber windowe St. Gregore the great and another, broken) and scutcheons with the pillar, the whip the dice and the cock. But after 1674 they were all broken — "downe went Dagon". Now no vestigea to be found.' There may have been intentional breaking but since Aubrey calls attention to the fact that one of the saints in his window was broken already, the quality called 'neglect' may have had its part in the ruin of the windows.

The really astonishing fact is, not that there is so little painted glass left, but that there is so much. I fancy, too, that the presentation of such paintings as that of St. Dunstan pulling the nose of the devil with a pair of tongs, which John Aubrey mentions as 'a very favourite subject' in his day, might be today regarded as a tedious curiosity if it were often repeated. Glass may have the quality of age which had never acquired that of beauty.

Anthony Wood (*History of the Colleges and Halls of Oxford*) made a careful inventory of the painted glass in position in his day, while the Royal Commission on Historical Monuments has preserved the record of what still exists (and there is good deal) in the churches and colleges of Oxford. A comparison is indicated to those who wish for accurate and authenticated knowledge.

But the story of the fate of painted windows may be learnt from any chronicle of men's deeds and misdeeds. John Byng of the *Torrington Diaries* had as keen an eye for stained glass in the eighteenth century as Aubrey in the seventeenth.

'Some curious stained glass was given from the windows here, to the Earl of Exeter at Burleigh, to put up in his (more modern) house! He should have had from me my eye-tooth first.'

There seem, however, to have been return journeys, for Mr. Byng also sets down that 'The eastern window (of the church) is of good old stained glass brought from a neighbouring old destroyed mansion'. Nor was Mr. Byng quite so guileless as the measure of his indignation warrants, for he writes:

'Just below the bridge, I entered a glazier's shop, in the hope of finding stained glass (a part of my pursuit) and was lucky enough to fill one pocket with fragments from Upwood Church, (of which the glazier is the repairer) offering for them so high a price as to confound the shop-boy — viz. sixpence.' It comes as no surprise therefore to read his later entry. 'Though the pillars and arches are of Saxon architecture, brasses and stained glass are gone.' Sometimes he records quite open pillaging as a matter which one might meet anywhere. 'The magnificent stained-glass of the chancel of the church has been removed by Lord F. the owner of the place . . . every pane of the wonderful stained glass has been pillaged and not replaced by any other.' There was surely never so curious a fate for church-windows as he records on another occasion, 'In the middle of an artificial lake is a hermitage finished with curious taste and trouble. Therein are several rooms, recesses and chapels, all lighted by old stained glass (*once in Tattershall Church*). The ornamental parts are of fir-cones, the *tables of polished horse bones*', etc.

In contrast to this method of disposing of old stained glass from churches, the old Puritan who broke 'Proud Beckett's glassy bones' seems inspired by a noble ardour.

RUINS OF
OSNEY ABBEY

128

XXXII

'The Unbought Grace'

If aught of oaten stop or pastoral song
May hope, chaste eve, to soothe thy modest ear,
Like thy own solemn springs,
Thy springs and dying gales.

'WHEN do you hear of him? Are there hopes of his recovery? or is he to pass the remainder of his life in misery and degradation, perhaps with complete consciousness of his calamity? . . . It is dreadful to consider that understanding may make its appearance and depart, that it may blaze and expire.' (*Dr. Johnson.*)

Within the variance of circumstance which the preceding passages suggest was lived and ended the short life of William Collins, who, like Shelley, seems to have a special association with Oxford, though, like Shelley, he left the university suddenly. Like Shelley, he was much beloved (though it was said of him that he didn't associate much). For Dr. Johnson he was 'such a man as Collins with whom I was delighted to converse and whom I still remember with tenderness'. For Hazlitt he was 'the only one of the minor poets of whom, if he had lived, it cannot be said that he might not have done the greatest things'. He was the poet who sustained the exalted music of Milton almost alone in his generation; yet he was also the poet whose sister 'evinced such an outrageous aversion to him, that she destroyed in a paroxysm of resentment all his papers and whatever remained of his enthusiasm for poetry as far as ever she could'. He was to commit absurdities as foolish as Shelley's under the shadow of tragedy as poignant as that of Cowper. His cousin Payne told him of his foolishnesses roundly, when he went visiting him with a feather cocked in his hat and wearing a fine suit. His duns told him so. Presumably his friends told him so at intervals and yet he remained for them 'such a man as Collins'. 'I tell you I love the fellow', said Dr. Johnson. He was to write 'How sleep the brave'. He was to receive a fortune 'too late to do anything but light him to an early grave', to leave behind him as legacy his own 'Unbought grace' as an English poet.

Long ago, one used to hear discussions as to how far this 'unbought grace' of the poet should excuse him from the unpleasant necessity of earning his living and paying his way. On one occasion I remember it was settled by the tart verdict of a young English professor, 'If the sky fell we should all catch larks'. The trouble is that that very unbought grace for which we value the poet is so delicate and ephemeral a quality that it may be lost in the very struggle to maintain it alive. Dr. Johnson was all for paying one's way, and he had himself surmounted the bitter waters of poverty, but he spoke from an acid experience when he said 'A man doubtful of his dinner, or trembling at a creditor is not much disposed to abstracted meditation or remote enquiries', and with all his affection for Collins he had many strictures upon his poetry and his habits of composition.

The facts of Collins's life are commonplace enough. He was born at Chichester and entered Winchester school. (The only known portrait of him belongs to his school-days.) He won a scholarship for New College but was not admitted for want of room, and a year later he entered as demy of Magdalen. He took his degree and then suddenly left Oxford without explanation other than can be found in his verse.

> 'O Nature boon, from whom proceed
> Each forceful thought, each prompted deed,
> If but from thee I hope to feel
> On all my heart imprint thy seal;
> Let some retreating cynic find
> Those oft-turned scrolls I leave behind,
> The sports and I this hour agree
> To rove thy scene-full world with thee.'

The youth with 'quick uncheated sight' became then an undergraduate in the scene-full world of London. That is all; like many other young men. It has happened before and since — the secret, slowly-growing discontent with mental development and opportunity in a given environment, and the apparently sudden determination to find elsewhere what the mind is seeking.

The instability of purpose with which his contemporaries reproached him — that he reached out after his grandiose schemes, planned them in exaltation and never did them — might be just the tale of any other young man not sure of himself and his direction. If the vigour of life had remained to him he might actually have carried

Footbridge over the Cherwell

them out. But what a good thing for posterity this really was. For the 'unbought grace' of Collins urged him to poetry and the writing of Odes, and an ode can be carried in the head to the rejoicing and renewing of the soul, while many volumes and histories of literature can be carried to and fro on the trolleys of Bodley's cellars to the great aching of backs. Since the poetry *was* written, his projected *Revival of the History of Learning* can be spared.

The life of Collins constantly returns to Oxford. His friends the Wartons lived there, and from time to time he came to rest there in ill-health. His ode on the Passions was set to music by William Hayes of Oxford and sung there in 1750 (reprinted with finale by another hand in 1811, and into Italian by an advocate Martelli) and it was from Oxford that he was finally removed to the asylum at Cowley.

The great bastions of the wall beneath Merton College Gardens serve now the purpose of the village pump of Oxford. I have heard astonishing matters in the sunshine which warms the old wooden benches and listened to more astounding opinions. But it is the memory of Collins under Merton Wall as Gilbert White saw him, struggling in the arms of three keepers who were trying to remove him to the asylum, which hurts like some poignant experience.

'How he got down to Oxford, I do not know, but I myself saw him under Merton Wall in a very affecting situation, struggling, and conveyed by force, in the arms of two or three men, towards the parish of St. Clement, in which was a house that took in such unhappy objects.'

For the greater part of his short life Collins was beloved, admired and helped. Dr. Johnson and Thomson were his friends. The two Wartons were his intimates. Yet no one (save possibly himself) even suspected the terrible failure of vital strength which seems to have been the ultimate cause of his brain malady.

Irresolution, instability, grandiose dreams, fell tragically into place. There are scenes recorded in the lives of English Poets which even now stop the heart's beating — Keats, panting out his life in that worst of all places for his malady, the broiling little flat on the Spanish Steps in Rome; Cowper's dark and haunted nights and Collins's sudden journey alone (he didn't associate much) into France to unhorse the spectre which already shook its spear at his side. He re-appeared, his brilliance and vigour gone for ever, his only reading, a child's school Bible. He continued to visit and to receive visits, but paroxysms there must have been, for it was the struggle beneath Merton Wall which shocked Gilbert White. He was removed from St. Clements to London and thence to his sister's at Chichester. His later days slipped by without the knowledge of his friends. 'How is poor Collins?' 'I have written to Collins but he does not reply.' Complete silence followed and then Collins was dead. His productive life had been five to six years, and from his journey to France nothing was harvested.

That the poetry of Collins holds aloof from personal emotions and passion and is all rather allegorical and impersonal is rather a modern, than a contemporary detraction. But to me, this shrinking from, or actual avoidance of personal feeling seems to echo the tragedy of Charles Lamb who was also accused of lightness and want of depth. The warning to avoid excessive personal emotion or excitement may very early have sounded in his brain. One takes — and in the case of Collins with great contentment — not what he did not, and perhaps could not give, but those golden and flute-like 'numbers' which he actually could and undeniably did give.

> 'Of these let others ask
> To aid some mighty task
> I only seek to find thy temperate vale.'

'The Noble Heart'

'The noble heart that harbours virtuous thought,
And is with child of glorious, great intent,
Can never rest until it forth have brought,
Th'eternal brood of glory excellent.'

THERE only remains now to write quiet and happy words upon the dead, those young dead, who passing gaily through our streets and being beloved, yet took from Life but their school-days and were gone. Mourning followed them, for it seemed that their evening had fallen at sunrise. Ardours they would have kindled were unlit. Knowledge they might have gathered and increased remained ungarnered. The continuity of learning as of laughter was broken. For them there was no scholar's ripening and their stature was immature. The inheritance of the past concerned them little, for their offering was of the future. Yet from the durable wisdom of the centuries they delayed to gather one fruit—the understanding of the noble heart. The continuity of Learning was broken, but the continuance of the noble heart held fast.